AN INTRODUCTION
TO THE
NEW HERMENEUTIC

AN INTRODUCTION
TO THE
NEW HERMENEUTIC

by Paul J. Achtemeier

The Westminster Press · Philadelphia

STANDARD BOOK NO. 664–20870–3

LIBRARY OF CONGRESS CATALOG CARD NO. 74–79666

62824

PUBLISHED BY THE WESTMINSTER PRESS®
PHILADELPHIA, PENNSYLVANIA

PRINTED IN THE UNITED STATES OF AMERICA

To Betty, Mark, and Marie,
in whose company life is joyful

Foreword

THERE APPEARS TO BE increasing recognition of the fact that the interpretation of Scripture is one of the key problems of contemporary theology. Its solution is necessary not only for theology in the more traditional sense but also for any kind of "ecumenical" theology within the "coming great church." It is therefore a question that needs serious reflection by any who are concerned with the Christian faith in the twentieth century.

One way of carrying on such reflection is represented by what has come to be known as the "new hermeneutic," a movement about which little is generally known other than the title. A number of books and articles have been written by followers and critics of the movement, but much of that material presumes some acquaintance with the problems and categories used by its proponents. Yet in order to be able to follow the discussion, some introduction is needed into the assumptions and structures of this way of reflecting on the problem of interpretation. Much of the discussion has occurred in the German language and remains as yet untranslated.

It may be noted at the outset that, although the term "new hermeneutic" has become the generally accepted term used to identify this movement, it is not the way in which this movement has designated itself in Germany, where it originated. The discussion there has been carried on more in terms of defining and working out a hermeneutical approach to Scripture and theology, and it tends to be referred to simply as *"Hermeneutik."* This particular theological discussion has been notable, however, for the fact that it has been carried on in dialogue between theologians of two countries and two languages, German and English. In the course of this discussion, American scholars have generally adopted the practice of using the word "hermeneutic" in the singular, when referring to this particular movement, and have reserved the plural form, "hermeneutics" for references to any other interest in interpretation to which such a general term is applicable. Because the term "new hermeneutic" has thus been generally adopted as the title for this way of doing theology in the English-speaking world, it will also be used here.

It is the purpose of this "introduction" to provide some at least of the orientation necessary so that the ongoing discussion may be intelligently followed. Although I have sought as much clarity as possible, I have tried to avoid oversimplification so that a fair picture of problems and proposed solutions may be gained. I have attempted, therefore, to sketch out the more immediate philosophical and theological background of the new hermeneutic, and have sought to treat its concerns in a thematic way. But the book is intended to introduce the reader to a way of thinking; it is not meant to serve as substitute for any further reading or reflection on this problem.

The discussion is divided into two major parts. The first deals with some of the background information that it is necessary to know if one is to understand why certain problems loom large for the proponents of the new hermeneutic. The second part contains an exposition of some of the major concerns with which this way of doing theology deals.

The exposition of the new hermeneutic is based primarily on the writing of two German theologians, Ernst Fuchs and Gerhard Ebeling. More emphasis has been placed on the former, since fewer of his works have been translated into English, and because he has pursued these problems in a more systematic and single-minded way. The book may also serve, for the time being at least, as an introduction to the thought of Ernst Fuchs.

These chapters are intended as exposition, and, for the most part, no attempt is made in them at evaluation or counter-argument. Such treatment has been reserved for a final chapter. Since much of the source material has appeared in German, I have from time to time had to translate portions of it in the body of the discussion. Unless otherwise indicated, I will have to assume responsibility for any translations, including New Testament passages, which appear within these pages.

I must also thank some of the many people who have listened patiently and asked probing questions over the past few years as I have sought to come to grips with the kind of thinking exposed in these pages. Several groups have afforded me the opportunity, through invitations to speak to them, to develop some of the material included here: Mr. Terry Burch, of the American Baptist Convention, who invited me to participate in the Open Theological Conference in the summer of 1967; the faculty and student body of St. Mary's Seminary in Baltimore, who included me in their annual series of lecturers for the 1967–1968 academic year; the professors of the Bible and theology departments of Pittsburgh Theological Seminary, who invited a paper on this topic. I must also express my thanks to Prof. George Kehm, of Pittsburgh Theological Seminary, who most graciously took time from his sabbatical leave to read the first draft of the chapters on Heidegger and Bultmann. Many of his valuable suggestions helped in shaping the discussion contained there, although he can hardly be held responsible for the use I made of his careful and illuminating comments. Finally, I must express my gratitude for the sympathetic ear and quick mind of my wife, who in this matter as in all else has been my true helpmeet.

P.J.A.

The Lancaster Theological Seminary
Lancaster, Pennsylvania

Contents

1

The Shape of the Problem

WHAT IS AT STAKE, when one broaches the problem of hermeneutics, is nothing less than the Biblical basis of Christian faith and theology. The hermeneutical question, as we shall approach it, concerns the fundamental problem of whether it is possible to put an ancient text (the Bible) at the basis of an affirmation of faith designed to be understood, and taken seriously, by modern man. Can a past event, and the text to which it gave birth, have any real significance for my life, now? That is the fundamental question about the possibility of current meaning for the Christian faith, and it is the question with which we want to deal in the pages of this book. For unless the Biblical text, and the kind of reality to which it points, can in fact give meaning to life in the present age, then the need for the Christian faith, to say nothing of Christian theology, has been seriously compromised, if not eliminated. The hermeneutical question, therefore, concerns itself with the possibility of Christian faith and theology in the modern world.

The meaning accorded to the word "hermeneutics" and the interest shown in it during the past three quarters of a century indicate the fate of the problem with which we want to deal. The word "hermeneutic" itself is derived from a Greek verb *hermēneuein*, which means "to speak," "to translate," or "to interpret." In theological discussion, hermeneutics traditionally belongs to a triad including exegesis, hermeneutics, and interpretation. In this group, exegesis normally meant determining what meaning the text had for its own author and intended readers, interpretation sought the meaning the text could have for the current age, and hermeneutics concerned the rules to apply in order to get from the former to the latter. Hermeneutics thus embraced theological reflection on the possibility and validity of finding valid contemporary meaning in ancient texts. In practice, however, the need for such reflection gradually was lost sight of, so that by the turn of the century, "hermeneutics" and "exegesis" often were used interchangeably.[1]

The fact that such reflection on how meaning—Biblical meaning—can be transferred from one historical and cultural context to another, entirely different context could come to be ignored provides an interesting commentary on the way theology has been carried on during the past few decades. Interest in this problem as the kind of problem with which theology can, indeed must, deal has only recently been revived.[2] Not that theology can ever be carried on without some solution to this problem. That solution may be more assumed than explicated, or it may be shaped on the basis of some traditional view upon which careful critical reflection has not been brought to bear. But one way or another, some solution to the hermeneutical problem is at work any time a sermon is preached or the Christian faith discussed. It is not a question of whether the problem ought to be solved; it is a question of whether the solution upon which a given theology and a given proclamation are based is a good solution or a bad one.

The question is therefore not whether or not theology should in any sense be understood in terms of hermeneutics, or interpretation. If theology is to make sense *now* about the meaning of Jesus Christ whose career took place *then*, it has in that moment engaged in a transfer of meaning. It has carried out a hermeneutic. Rather, the question is whether that hermeneutic, or the principle on the basis of which it has been carried out, is to be the object of deliberate theological reflection, or whether it is to be assumed and allowed to operate without benefit of theological clarification. The reemergence of hermeneutics as a concern for serious theological reflection indicates that for a part of the theological world, at any rate, the answer to that question has been decided. Hermeneutics must be given serious theological consideration.

There are several reasons for this reemergence from theological obscurity. It is one of the great unsolved problems with which the era of "liberal" theology grappled, with its concern over how much of the historic faith was credible to the modern age. The problem was never really solved. The fate of the world intervened in the form of economic and political catastrophe and summoned theology to other, more pressing tasks. Or so it seemed. The sheer theological brilliance of the work of Karl Barth forced theology to grapple with, and reflect on, other kinds of issues. To be sure, a hermeneutical principle was at work in the theology of Karl Barth, but it was itself not accorded full status as a theological issue. But unresolved problems have a way of refusing to lie dormant for long, and it ought to be cause of no surprise that it has again thrust itself to the center of our attention.

It is, to put it simply, a problem that dare not be ignored. Until this problem is solved, until some clarity has been achieved concerning how the Bible may legitimately be appropriated in the modern era, theology will continue to thrash around, casting up all manner of solutions ranging from the bizarre to the naïve, from resolute "fundamentalism" to the "theological" affirmation that God is dead. Serious theological work will probably not be able to be gotten under way again until the hermeneutical problem is solved. It is little wonder, then, that it has emerged from its obscurity.

A second reason for its reemergence is rooted in the nature of the Christian faith itself. The fact that writings completed some two millennia ago are still used by the Christian faith as its normative Scripture means that the problem of the understanding of one historical period by another is built into the Christian faith. As long as theology takes seriously the New Testament witness that the decisive revelation of God occurred in the career of Jesus of Nazareth, a first-century Jew, it will be forced to grapple with the problem of how the past may legitimately be said to exercise any normative influence over the present. As long as the Christian faith understands itself as in any significant way rooted to the historic event of Jesus of Nazareth, it will never be able to carry on theology for an extended period of time before the hermeneutical problem makes itself felt; indeed, forces itself into the foreground.

A third reason for the reemergence of the hermeneutical problem as a pressing concern for theology is to be found in the modern crisis in confidence in the possibility and validity of historical knowledge.[3] It would be fair to say that the one key element that characterizes the modern period and that makes it unique in the history of human intellectual development is the discovery of the historically relative nature of human truth and the historically conditioned nature of human culture and human understanding, and the corresponding inability to assume that what was true in the past must inevitably be true for the present as well. It is no longer sufficient, in order to prove a thing true, to prove that it has traditionally been regarded as true. An abyss has opened up between historical periods, which makes understanding of one age by another an acute intellectual problem.

The idea of the relativity of historical reality, understood in its broadest terms, received its present development in the nineteenth century, with the emergence of historical "science" as an intellectual discipline. Much can be said for and against that development, but for our purposes we shall limit ourselves to the observation that one result of our heritage of that intellectual movement consists in the fact that it is now regarded as self-evident and axiomatic that all intellectual achievements are limited by the historical period in which they took form and flourished. With that there comes the realization that it is impossible ever really to transcend the limits of one's historical period, impossible ever completely to cease being the child of one's own age. To take history seriously in this way is in effect to question the possibility of direct, undistorted knowledge of another historical period. Even when I make the effort to understand, say, a document from the first century in its own terms, it is still I as a twentieth-century person who do that. To take this insight seriously is to have brought home to one the realization that he can see nothing except through historically conditioned eyes. It is this insight which makes it impossible for a modern painter of a scene from antiquity to clothe the people in contemporary dress, and set them against the background of contemporary architecture, something quite possible for artists of another age, e.g., such fifteenth-century painters as Sassetta, Crivelli, or Fra Filippo Lippi. If we want to portray ancient events, we *know* that we cannot clothe them in the dress of the twentieth century. It is precisely this *knowing* which stamps us as the heirs of the discovery of the relativity of historical periods.

To affirm that this insight in its turn is the characteristic of our age, that for us to look at things historically is to look at them from within the (historical) confines of our own period, does nothing to discredit the insight into historical relativity. Indeed, it confirms it. As children of our age (itself a phrase drawing on the insight into historical relativity), we are compelled to see things from our own, unique, historical perspective, and, what is more, to be aware that we must do so. It is small wonder, in that kind of age, that the problem of history, and its understanding, would arise within theology.

These insights, which raise the problem of the place of history in theology, also give that problem its configuration. On the one hand, we can no longer assume that our way of understanding the nature of the Christian faith is identical to the way it was understood by the New Testament authors of the first and second centuries, simply because we are much too aware of the historical changes that have taken place in the intervening time. We simply belong to an entirely different "world." On the other hand, we cannot jettison the historical problem altogether, and live simply on some kind of "eternal" spiritual resources, be-

cause the nature of the Christian faith is such that if its historic
roots are lost, it ceases to become identifiably Christian.[4] Thus,
at one and the same time are given the necessity for some kind
of interpretation of the Biblical texts, and the problem inherent
in any attempt to be sure that a given interpretation comports
with the original intention of its author in any significant way.
This is the kind of problem with which the new hermeneutic
sets out to deal.

All of this is not to say, of course, that the discovery of the
need for interpretation of the Biblical writings is recent or modern. The history of Christian theology is, in a sense, the history
of the attempt to find contemporary relevance, in any given age,
in the Biblical writings and in the traditions of the Christian
faith. It does mean, however, that a new awareness of the pit-
falls of careless or naïve interpretation has in fact awakened. As
one scholar has observed, "Today, hermeneutical philosophy has
made exegetes self-conscious about their presuppositions."[5]

It would perhaps be helpful, at this point, to look very briefly
at some of the kinds of presuppositions that have operated in
past attempts at interpretation, so that we may gain a perspective on the problem in general, and prepare ourselves in a broad
way to undertake the investigation of the new hermeneutic.

For the transfer of meaning to occur, for the "hermeneutical
situation" to exist, there must be some point of contact between
interpreter and text. Without such contact, no meaning can be
transferred. The contact may be as tenuous as simply a knowledge of the language in which a text is written, or it may be so
total as to include the interpreter's whole being. This latter is
the case, for example, when we read a local newspaper. We do
not raise the question of how understanding is possible in that
situation. We simply understand it, because we share the same
world with it. Our contact is total. When such total immersion
in the same linguistic and cultural world is lacking, however, the
problem arises whether or not the text is understood. Then the
question must be raised about the kind of contact between us
and this ancient text, as in the case of the Bible, which makes

understanding possible. In any hermeneutical situation, that point of contact exists, whether as subject of conscious reflection or not.

That point of contact may, for example, consist in the assumption that the structure of reality is always and everywhere basically the same.[6] The early Christian Apologists would be an example of that, with their theologies based on the concept of the "logos." Using that logos as the tool, they want to show that the history of intellectual endeavor, following the lines of common reason and the structure of reality, leads to the same conclusions as those embodied in the Christian faith. Valid thinking in any age, so they argue, which in turn is grounded in the structure of reality, finds its model and best expression in the teachings of the faith. A second example of such a hermeneutical point of contact would be the theology of Origen, for whom similarly the essential meaning of Scripture, and the revelation it contains, correspond to the essential structure of reality. And that in turn determines the structure of human understanding. When human understanding functions correctly, it will find the truth in Scripture, which must correspond to the structure of reality. That truth is not always evident on the surface, however. Indeed, argues Origen, to take all Scripture at its surface meaning, i.e., in a literal sense, is to open oneself to confusion and untruth. To get at the truth beyond the (unworthy) literal sense, therefore, Origen employed allegory as his hermeneutical tool. Allegorical interpretation for Origen is thus not a device for performing arbitrary exegesis, but is rather the tool necessary to get at the intention of Scripture in those places where the literal meaning lacks edification, or is unworthy of the Holy Spirit. Allegory, functioning properly, will allow the human intellect to discern those elements of revelation in Scripture which correspond to the structure of reality, which in turn underlies and structures human thinking. In both instances, Origen and the Apologists, Scripture may be understood because the structure of reality, which shapes human thought, also structures the revelation contained in Scripture.

Where such confidence in man's ability to fathom the structure of reality is not so strong, another kind of contact may be assumed. For example, it may be contact on the basis of traditional continuity. Such continuity can be posited of a traditional confession of faith, as in the case of the early Catholic Church which developed the criterion of true faith as that which has always and everywhere been held by everyone, a view that was in operation long before it received its explicit formulation by Vincent of Lérins. This idea of a rule of faith, a *regula fidei*, on the basis of which Scripture is to be understood, is already operative in a Clement of Rome, with his appeal not to abandon established ways, or in an Ignatius of Antioch, with his appeal to the office of Bishop as the indispensable guarantor of sound faith. In each of these cases, the guarantee of legitimate interpretation of Scripture is its conformity to the sum total of Christian doctrine, and the rule becomes: what does not agree with the "faith" cannot be a legitimate interpretation. To prove a thing traditional is thus to prove it true.

A similar impulse was at work in the period of Protestant Orthodoxy of the sixteenth and seventeenth centuries. Instead of appealing to a *regula fidei*, they spoke of *analogia fidei*, the "analogy of faith," by which they meant that all elements of the faith and of Scriptural interpretation must cohere with one another in an all-embracing theological whole. Where Scripture was unclear, the analogy of faith would indicate the way the interpretation must be made. The appeal here was to coherence rather than tradition, as in the case of the *regula fidei*, but in both instances the structure of faith makes interpretation possible. While the orthodox theologians called upon the inner testimony of the Holy Spirit as that which made valid understanding of Scripture possible, in practice it tended to be the coherence of their theological systems which threw light on Scripture. The "faith" of the "analogy of faith" tended to be the theological system of a given author. In both of these instances, therefore, that which makes understanding of Scripture possible is the total configuration of the Christian faith.

Another possibility, this one more recent, sees the hermeneutical situation grounded in the essentially unchanging structures of human nature. Although this is never explicitly stated by Schleiermacher, it is clear that this is precisely the presupposition on the basis of which he operates. In his lectures on hermeneutics, Schleiermacher makes it clear that he thinks it is necessary to know more than the literal sense in order to understand Scripture.[7] To understand any author, he argued, one must seek to penetrate the inner workings of that author's mind. One must ask of a text: What caused the author to choose just these words and phrases, instead of any of the others open to him? In this way, one must attempt to re-create in one's own mind the mental processes of the author that resulted in the text's being written as it now stands before us. This method of understanding and interpretation will be possible only if one assumes that all men operate intellectually in fundamentally the same way. There is, argued Schleiermacher, a universal "type-consciousness" in man, which simply means that the consciousness of all beings of the human "type" functions in the same manner. We can thus understand another by re-creating in our own self-consciousness the self-consciousness of the author. Such penetration of the inner workings of another mind obviously would not be possible unless the basic structures of human nature, including the mental processes, remained fundamentally unaffected by the culture and linguistic formulations of the period in which a man lived.

Interestingly enough, this is precisely the hermeneutical situation presumed by the young Karl Barth when he wrote his commentary on Romans. In the preface written in 1921 for the second edition of that commentary, he explains how he interprets the text: "Intelligent comment means that I am driven on till the document seems hardly to exist as a document; till I have almost forgotten that I am not its author; till I know the author so well that I allow him to speak in my name and am even able to speak in his name myself."[8] This same kind of presupposition seems also to underlie Rudolf Bultmann's contention that the understanding of existence seeking expression in first-century mythological terms is a valid way of understanding existence in the twentieth century. Since the world has changed radically in the intervening years, can such a method of approach be possible except on the supposition of the unchanging nature of human nature?[9]

These are some ways, then, in which an attempt has been made to understand and apply the hermeneutical approach, which makes such understanding possible. There are, of course, other ways and other solutions. One can, for example, ignore the possibility of any difficulty at all, and go on blithely under the assumption that whatever the (first-century, Hellenistic-Jewish, New Testament) text suggests to us (twentieth-century, Western) men now is its true intention.[10] Or the difficulty can be bridged by an appeal to church tradition and sacraments as the elements that put us into immediate contact with the (historical) reality to which the New Testament points, and then argue that as a result any talk of the hermeneutical need for "bridging a gap" need not be entertained.[11] Or it is possible simply to assume that what had meaning for man once must continue to have the same meaning in the same terms, since the Spirit that informs the Bible is the Eternal Spirit. Therefore, since what were key problems for first-century man remain the key problems for us, and in the same way, those solutions can be applied without raising the knotty problem of the historically conditioned nature of man and world.[12] There can be no denying the persuasive force which that kind of view is capable of generating, and which, on occasion, it still does. But for those who seek some way of measuring at what point the intention of Scripture ceases and the expositor's own interpretative theology begins, the method is not satisfactory. And if we cannot make Paul or Abraham contemporary figures simply by fiat, neither can we become Hebrews of the second millennium B.C. or Hellenistic Jews of the first century. The modern insight into historical relativity has, as we have urged above, rendered that impossible.

If then it would seem impossible to remain faithful to the historic roots of the Christian faith, and acknowledge their normative value, without at the same time acknowledging the problem this creates in the realm of historical knowledge, any discussion of the hermeneutical problem will have to take into account the historicality of man, his existence and his world. If the nature of historical reality is such that each age must understand anew, and in its own terms, the meaning the Biblical events and records have for that age, and if such understanding is possible only within the framework of the age that seeks to understand, where are we to turn for guidance in undertaking this task for our age? If, as James Robinson has written, "there is no haven free from the storms of temporal existence into which the Biblical meaning can once for all be safely carried and stored," where do we look to find a clue concerning the meaning the Bible may have for us now?[13] What kind of herme- neutical situation will operate effectively for those who have seen the yawning abyss of historical relativity swallow up all naïve attempts to arrive at a "one to one" correlation of Biblical man and world to modern man and world? Where do they turn when they are not sure that the structure of reality does in fact inform human thought in such a way as to make it readily, or even not so readily, discernible? When the Reforma- tion has pointed out to them the theological dangers inherent in a reliance on sacrament and tradition to put them into direct contact with New Testament realities? When an appeal to the Holy Spirit as guarantor of the validity of a given interpretation stands under the Johannine injunction to test the spirits, since not all are to be believed? When such testing leaves unanswered the question: To what extent has the intention of the Holy Spirit, expressing itself through man, been forced into another mold by one who could not, or would not, bend to that inten- tion?

One recent attempt to come to grips with the problems is represented by the "new hermeneutic." It is a method of ap- proaching the problem of interpretation which has developed in full awareness of the historicality of human existence, and which seeks to find a viable way to cross the gap in meaning between the New Testament and our time. The new hermeneutic is important if for no other reason than that it does take seriously those elements to which we have pointed as constituting the problem of interpretation for our time. In the course of our exposition of this theological movement, some of the issues will become apparent with which any theology must deal, if that theology seeks to speak meaningfully to modern man about the Christian faith. Whatever one may think of the solution proposed by the new hermeneutic, a solution based on language as the key to man's existence as man, and therefore the key to man's attempt to understand himself and his world, this way of approaching the problem merits a serious hearing because it has hold of what appears to be the key problem for valid Christian theology and proclamation in the twentieth century.

We shall therefore attempt, in the chapters of this book, to outline the background and substance of the problem as it appears to the new hermeneutic, with the hope that it will aid others in understanding the issues that are being debated by its proponents. But even more, the purpose of the book will have been served if it leads others to reflect theologically on this vital problem of the understanding and interpreting of the Christian faith in the only way open to us—and that is, as men of the twentieth century.

PART ONE

BACKGROUND

THEOLOGICAL MOVEMENTS such as the new hermeneutic do not spring full-blown into existence. They develop from a variety of roots and represent the accumulated theological work, whether in positive or negative evaluation of it, of many years and many men. Any possibility of understanding such a movement will therefore, to some extent at least, depend upon some knowledge of those historical roots. We must therefore sketch at least some of the intellectual currents that have contributed to the formation and development of the new hermeneutic.

The roots of the movement reach back to the work of Schleiermacher and Dilthey, surely, but for our purposes they lie more directly in the thought of Martin Heidegger and Rudolf Bultmann, from whose works substance is drawn both for problems to be dealt with and for the method to be used. We must, therefore, in this first part, examine briefly the major contours of the philosophical thinking of Heidegger, and then, again very briefly, look at the way Bultmann attempted to formulate a theology understandable to modern man by drawing on resources furnished by Heidegger's thought. Because of the great importance attached to language by the new hermeneutic, it has also seemed appropriate to include a chapter dealing with the way man perceives the world around him and the part that language appears to play. The chapter should give the reader added perspective from which to evaluate the kind of claim made by the new hermeneutic on behalf of language.

2
Martin Heidegger — I

ATTEMPTING TO FOLLOW the thought of Martin Heidegger is rather like trying to follow a path that gradually disappears as it leads one into the densest part of the forest. Perhaps the surest indication that one has not understood him would lie in the claim that one could treat his thought as a totality, in one or two chapters, and we have no intention of making such a claim! Yet the main lines of his thought can be discerned, even if at the price of some simplification, and the attempt must be made to discern them, since so much of the style and manner of Heidegger's thought has been of great importance in the development of the new hermeneutic.[1]

Martin Heidegger was born in 1889 in southern Germany, began his serious study in the area of theology, and then continued in philosophy. He became a professor in the department of philosophy in the University of Marburg in 1923, and remained there until 1928, when he accepted a call to the University of Freiburg. During his career at Marburg, he was a colleague of Rudolf Bultmann, who held a chair in the department of theology (New Testament). Heidegger was rector of the University of Freiburg in 1933, and for a time openly expressed support for the National Socialist party, which had then just come to power. Although he soon ceased to be a vocal sympathizer, he has been severely castigated for that early support. In recent years, he has retired to a house in the Black Forest, lecturing and writing occasionally. Several of his works have appeared in English translation, but the complexity of his thought, compounded by the complexity and novelty of his use of German, makes translation a particularly difficult task. The peculiar English employed by those who write about Heidegger, along with their liberal use of hyphens, is the result of his use of the German language.

The fundamental question with which Heidegger sets out to deal is the question of "Being." In the discussion that follows, we shall employ a distinction, used by Wm. J. Richardson, among others, between "Being" and "being." This corresponds to a fundamental distinction in Heidegger's thought between "being as such" (*Sein*) and "a being" (*Seiendes*). When we refer to *Sein*, or "being as such," we shall capitalize the word "Being"; when we refer to *Seiendes*, or "a being," we shall write the word as "being." This distinction is pivotal for Heidegger, and this seems as good a way as any to convey the distinction in English. Thus, a "being" is anything that is, while "Being" is that by which it is, that which keeps it from non-Being. The problem facing such a discussion is apparent already in the clarification of terms: How can there "be" non-Being? But how else can it be expressed? Our language itself bears witness to the complexity of the problem.

We must also warn against any tendency on the part of the reader to identify "Being" with God. That is *not* what Heidegger has in mind. Heidegger is not Paul Tillich; "Being-itself" for Heidegger is *not* another way to describe God. As a philosopher, Heidegger apparently feels that it is not in his province to ask about God, nor to use God as an "answer." Heidegger remains a philosopher. He does not become a theologian, and any attempt to equate what he means by Being with what the Christian means by God can only lead to a basic misunderstanding of what he is speaking about.

Basic to the task, then, to which Martin Heidegger gives himself is the question of "Being." He asks: What is there in everything that keeps it from sliding into nothing? What is the difference between what is, and what is not? What is it that characterizes all things that are, which is the reason that there "is" something, and not simply nothing? Heidegger's problem is therefore ontology, i.e., the nature and structure of Being. He is careful to distinguish between "beings," i.e., things that are, and "Being," i.e., that by which they are, and this distinction must be kept in mind, if one is to grasp his thinking. If at times his language becomes poetic, at times obscure, it is at least partly due to the subtlety of the questions with which he seeks to deal.

The task, then, is to "think Being." It is to pursue that sudden, eerie insight that there is something, rather than simply nothing. Why should that be so? Philosophy was born when a man suddenly pondered the possibility of non-Being, and asked: Why is there something? Why not nothing? What is it that separates Being from non-Being, which all beings share yet which is itself not a being? Heidegger's task is to follow the implications of that single insight, with which Western philosophy began. But to ask it steadfastly means never to make Being into a being of some sort or other. Being is neither a being nor the sum total of all beings. To remain true to the primal question is therefore to respect the "ontological difference," i.e., the difference between Being and beings. Being can obviously never be confronted except as the Being of some being; it does not exist apart from beings, but Being is not identical with any being or with all beings. The task, then, is to ponder Being. It is to respond to this primal insight of philosophy.

Yet there has developed over the years a kind of thinking that makes it all but impossible to respect the ontological difference, a kind of thinking that all but guarantees the confusion of Being and beings. That kind of thinking is called "metaphysics." Metaphysics developed, Heidegger argues, when man lost the insight into the wonder of Being, and began to take Being for granted, and to go on to deal with the various kinds of beings, ordering and classifying them. That is, man closed himself to a response to Being, and began to deal with beings. Ontology, i.e., wonder at Being, thus becomes metaphysics, i.e., contemplation of the totality of beings. At that point, beings become the "objects" of thought which the "subject" then thinks. In this way, thought and logic have come to be dominated by the "subject-object split." This has three consequences. In the first place, by separating subject from object, it erects a barrier between man and his world, so that man is never sure, theoretically at least, about what is "out there." Perhaps it is mere illusion; perhaps my subjective knowledge of the world bears little or no relation to objective reality. This then becomes the question that dominates Western philosophy, and is given classic expression, though not solved, by Descartes. Secondly, by placing the "objects" under the power of the "subject" which then classifies and organizes them into various categories, this kind of thinking really removes thought from the possibility of real encounter with reality. If something is observed that does not fit any category, it is either ignored or explained away. Thus, knowledge is hopelessly subjectivized, because it must meet the test of the subject's categories before it is recognized as true. In that case, any chance of contact, through thought, with Being is forever lost. But thirdly, such logical thinking, which structures all thought in terms of accepted categories, and which can only deal with objects, i.e., beings, can never come to terms with non-Being, which is part of the primal experience of Western thought. Non-Being cannot become an object of thought, since it is not any kind of object, or being. Therefore, metaphysics, dominated by logical thought, is totally unequipped to deal with the basic experience of philosophy, i.e., the wonder at Being, that things are, instead of there being simply non-Being, nothing.

If one is to think Being, therefore, one must overcome metaphysics, one must "step back" to a point prior to the subject-object split, and its organized form, logic. This is the task of the kind of fundamental ontology Heidegger wants to undertake. If he speaks, therefore, of "pre-logical thought," he does not mean simply arbitrary, capricious thinking. He means a kind of thought that makes it possible to respond to the ontological difference, to the wonder at Being, a kind of thinking that will let Being and, thus, beings be what they are, without forcing them into certain categories. The task to which Heidegger sets himself, therefore, is to reach a point in thinking where the ontological difference can be allowed to stand, and to dictate the form of thought. In this sense metaphysics, as a way of thinking that itself dictates the manifestations Being can have, must be overcome, so that the task of thinking Being can be undertaken again.

If this task is to be successfully undertaken, however, it is obvious that some method will have to be employed that at least gives promise of yielding suitable results. It will have to be a method free of the kind of built-in restrictions that Heidegger finds within any method predicated on the subject-object split, i.e., the "scientific method." Since ontology is to concern itself with Being, and since Being does not exist apart from beings, but is not identical with their totality, it is obvious that the method will have to allow the Being of beings to come to light. This "allowing to come to light" will then have to be descriptive of the method to be used. We cannot impose any a priori categories upon the manifestation of Being, on pain of reintroducing the subject-object split. The method will therefore have to allow Being to manifest itself as it is; it will have to be descriptive. That is precisely what "phenomenology" is. It is the description of things as they present themselves to the one who describes. Therefore, Heidegger asserts, "ontology is possible only as phenomenology."[2] But more than a "surface description" is necessary. If Being revealed itself as it truly is, there would be no need for a careful description to allow it to manifest itself as it truly is. Thus, phenomenological analysis must have as its goal the bringing to light of that which is hidden to man in his ordinary intercourse with the world, but which does in fact underlie all such intercourse. And if ordinary intercourse is described in ordinary language, then phenomenological analysis will have to have recourse to extraordinary language, if more than the ordinary is to be brought to light. The task of phenomenology is therefore to penetrate behind the facade of everydayness and ordinary appearance, in order to lay bare, in appropriate language, that which lies hidden within the ordinary, i.e., to find Being in the midst of beings. Thus the method conforms to the task: so to penetrate the ordinary beings that that which is their (hidden) ground, namely Being, may come to light. To anticipate some later vocabulary, the purpose of phenomenology is to "retrieve" the foundational experience of all thought and language, the experience of Being, which has been obscured by further developments in thought and language, in this instance, metaphysics.

We have the task and the method; now where do we begin? Rather obviously, with the ontological difference, i.e., difference between beings and Being. Yet that difference is the discovery made by man. It is not until man raises the question of the difference between beings and Being that ontology is possible. Therefore, the point of departure ought to be the being that raises the question about Being, i.e., man. Furthermore, if man asks the question about Being, then man must stand in some special relationship to Being, and in that case, the place at which to begin seems again to be: man. Therefore, Heidegger begins his analysis of Being by attempting to discern, phenomenologically, the Being of man.

We have already seen that Being, as Heidegger conceives it, is that which holds beings forth against non-Being; it is that which allows things to be what they are. Being is, therefore, in a sense, a "lighting-process," whereby beings "shine forth" as what they are. But for this kind of "non-concealment" to occur, there must be some place where it can happen, just as a light bulb, for example, needs a "place" to shine. This place, for Heidegger, is man. Man is thus the place were Being "comes to light," and apart from man there would be no Being at all, as Heidegger understands it. We must recall that Being is not the sum total of beings. Rather, it is that process by which beings unveil themselves. And if it is true that there can be no beings apart from Being, it is also true that unless there were a "place" where the question of Being could be raised, Being itself would remain submerged in beings, and never be allowed to come to light. Because it is man who alone can perceive the "ontological difference," i.e., the difference between beings and Being, man is the place where Being can be comprehended, or "come to light." Therefore, Being in a sense "needs" man in order to emerge as itself. And this, for Heidegger, is precisely man's task— to allow Being to emerge, to comprehend Being so that it can come to light. For this reason, Heidegger adopts the word *Dasein* for human being. *Da-sein* means to be at a place (literally "there-being"), and Heidegger uses it to mean that human existence (*sein*) is the place (*da*) where Being occurs. If Being as the lighting-process does not occur in man, it does not occur at all. Man's task, therefore, is to allow the illumination to occur. Man's task is to think Being.

That, in turn, means that man as truly man, i.e., as "there-being," is constituted by an event, namely, the event of the comprehension of Being. When one speaks of "human nature," for Heidegger, one speaks thus not of an entity, but of an occurrence, of something that must happen again and again. If Being needs man to come to light, then man also needs Being in order to achieve himself, i.e., in the comprehension of Being. Man is thus driven to comprehend Being in order to become, and remain, man. But that is a task which can never be completed, once for all. Therefore, man always has his task before him. And if that task is the comprehension of Being, ever anew, and if man is so constituted that this is a possibility for him, then man *is* his own potentiality. Man *is* the possibility of comprehending Being. But if man always has the potentiality of further comprehension of Being, then man is always more than he at present is; he can never fully realize his potentiality. Thus, man transcends himself in the possibility of comprehending Being, which is his nature. Man must therefore comprehend Being to realize himself as a man, and thus he is responsible for his own existence. But man did not choose that sort of task for himself. Rather, he has been "thrown" into human existence that has such a character. Man is therefore finite (limited by being thrown into a specific being) transcendence (his possibilities always transcend what he has at any given moment realized).

But how does this work itself out in human existence? If man is a being, thrown among beings, with the task of comprehending Being, how does that take place? To answer this, Heidegger analyzes the way man functions. He seeks to determine, by looking at the phenomenon of man (remember his method is phenomenology, i.e., a description of what appears), what the structural elements of human existence are. Such structural elements he calls "existentials." What is it, then, that makes man what he is, and causes him to function as he does; or, to ask it another way, what are these existentials? What are the structural elements in man that lie at the base of all man is and does?

One of the structural elements of human existence, surely, is the fact that no man exists in a vacuum. Man lives in relationship to other beings, human and non-human. Man, in other words, cannot have his being as man in total isolation. One structural element of human nature, therefore, is being-in-the-world. By "world," however, Heidegger does not mean the sum total of everything "out there." "World," as it functions for man, means that part of the world with which man comes into contact, and which influences him. Therefore, Heidegger uses the term "world" to mean the sum total of interrelationships within which man lives, and within which he finds, and assigns, meaning. World is thus a "referential totality," i.e., that reality in reference to which man exists. Thus, world means more than simply "objects." It also comprises the characteristics of human interaction, e.g., love, hate, desire, and the like. These are as real for man as a table or a turtle, and they are part of the world within which he lives. Man thus becomes man in traffic with his environment, and that traffic is a constitutive part of his nature. When man comes to understand himself, therefore, he understands himself in terms of his "world," as Heidegger uses that word.

This points to another characteristic of human existence, namely, that man always exists in relationship to himself. That is, man is capable of understanding himself, of standing off, as it were, and looking at himself. That means, put another way, that man is capable of understanding himself as man, but more, he is not a man until he does understand himself as man. Self-understanding is thus another structural element that makes man man, and Heidegger can describe that element by saying human nature is constituted by being related to itself in terms of its own self-understanding.

Here another characteristic of man has cropped up: understanding. Man would not be man without the capacity to understand himself and his world. Indeed, without this structural element, man would not be able to perform his task, which is the comprehension of Being. Another structural element, closely related to understanding, is the power of expression, which in concrete form is language. Man would not be man without this capacity to communicate. Indeed, as Heidegger continued to develop his thought, this becomes the most important of all the structural elements of man. "The essence of man rests in language," he writes; "it is language alone which enables man to become that kind of living entity which he is as man."[3]

It is further characteristic of man that what he encounters in the world awakens in him some sort of reaction: joy, sorrow, fear, contentment, and the like. That is, man always exists in some sort of "mood" in his traffic with the world. It is an inevitable concomitant to his openness to the world, and is another structural element in his being as man.

It would be a mistake, however, to think that man can exist as man without any one of these structures (of which we have named only a few) in operation. In fact, they operate as a unity, each influencing the other, as man operates as a unity, and can be separated only for purposes of analysis. But if man functions as a unity, is there any way to describe that unity? Yes, says Heidegger, it can be described as man's "concernful" dealing with the world. It is man's "concern," his "care," to salvage himself, to continue to be. But this concern is always the concern of a man who always has his task before him, who may fail in that task, and thus may cease to exist truly as a man. This threat of his own non-being means that man experiences this "care" or "concern" in his normal existence as "anxiety." If concern expresses the unity of the structural elements in man, and that concern is experienced as anxiety, then anxiety is that element in which man is disclosed to himself as a unity.[4]

All of this has two very important consequences. In the first place, if it is true that man becomes man in traffic with other beings, and cannot understand himself except in terms of these relationships, then the problem of how man "in here" comes into contact with things "out there" so that he may achieve knowledge about them has been shown to rest on a false understanding of man. Man is not man except in traffic with what is "out there"; thus human nature itself presupposes a relationship with them, and the problem of how the "subject" may be truly related to the "object" is answered in the very way man becomes man. He cannot become, and continue to be, man except in contact with that world. The problem rests on a falsely abstract view of human nature. However trivial such a consequence may seem, it does contain an insight into the way understanding takes place. Since, as we saw, man becomes man in traffic with his world, he already has a (prior) contact with reality which will later become conscious and explicit in the form of "understanding." "Understanding" is thus an interpretation of a relationship to reality which existed prior to its becoming conscious. Understanding and the language by which it is expressed, therefore, perform a "hermeneutical" function, i.e., they interpret the reality with which man comes into contact. The very structure of understanding thus presumes that wherever understanding takes place, some prior relationship to what is understood will have existed. This prior relationship Heidegger calls "pre-understanding," and "understanding" is the process of explicating and clarifying this pre-understanding. But the clearer one understands his prior relationship to reality, the clearer it will become to him that the understanding he has achieved needs further clarification as an interpretation of this relationship. Thus, un-

derstanding, as the interpretation of the prior relationship, allows one to see that relationship in a new light, which leads to
a reinterpretation of it, which sheds still more light on the prior
relationship, which shows the need for further clarification, and
so on. This circular structure which functions wherever understanding occurs Heidegger calls the "hermeneutical circle." It is
one consequence of Heidegger's analysis of the structure of human existence.

There is, however, a second consequence to be drawn from
that analysis. If man becomes man in traffic with his environment, and if as a result understanding occurs only in terms of
prior relationships, then it follows that man will understand
himself in terms of his environment. Seen in the light of the
way man conducts his life, this will mean that man allows himself to be told by the world around him what he ought to be.
That is, he will conform to his environment. He will simply
become an expression of what "they," the faceless, anonymous
mass, think a man ought to be. Man is then not a self, but an
expression of everyday commonness, an expression of what
"they" think he ought to be. Seen in the light of man's ontological task, i.e., he must be the place where Being can come to
expression, it means that man thinks of himself in terms of the
beings he confronts in the world. He thus loses Being in the
midst of beings. He becomes so involved with beings that he
does not perform the task given him, namely, thinking Being,
and so he is not really the "there-being" (i.e., the there of Being,
the place where Being emerges) that he ought to be. When man
does not perform the task which alone constitutes his true Being as man, he is living "inauthentically." He lives in "forgetfulness of Being," as unaware of non-Being as he is unaware of
his own finitude. He lives therefore in "fallenness of Being."

We must again caution against reading any kind of religious
connotations into what is an ontological analysis. There is no
moral judgment connected with "fallenness of Being," since
there is no other way man can become man save through traffic
with his environment, and no other way he can understand him-

self except in terms of that traffic. More specifically, this idea is not to be equated with the Biblical idea of the "Fall of Man." Whether or not Heidegger would have analyzed man in the way he does, and would have chosen the terminology he has chosen, had he not begun his intellectual life studying for the priesthood is a question that we may simply allow to rest.

That man lives in "fallenness of Being," furthermore, has as a consequence the fact that the way in which all the structural elements of human nature function will be affected by this state in which man finds himself. His understanding of himself will be drawn not from his true Being (the "there" where Being emerges), but from the beings with which he is engaged in the world. This kind of inauthentic being will be characterized by curiosity, for example, rather than by the attempt to think Being; by ambiguity, instead of by comprehension based on the fundamental association with Being through beings; by loquacity, instead of a clear expression of what is comprehended. Language then becomes banal, and ceases to respond to the lighting-process of Being. It becomes simply "what 'they' say." The self thus abdicates its responsibility to be a self and abandons itself to the "they" who set the general pattern everyone is "expected" to follow. This results in a certain tranquillity, in which there is no need to wrestle with any decisions; one simply accepts and does what "they" prescribe, and do.

Yet through it all, the self remains inauthentic, and despite the tranquilizing effect of the reliance on "them," there is a basic sense of emptiness. The self is dimly aware of its pre-occupation with beings at the expense of Being. This emptiness begets a restlessness, which seeks more and more to lose itself in simply "doing." But this can only result in increasing alienation of the inauthentic self from its true task, and its true self. The structural element by which man is aware of himself as a unity, namely anxiety, becomes now a nameless dread, which leads to more frantic activity in the effort to quell the uneasiness of a self leaving undone its basic task: to become the place where Being comes to light.

It is precisely this effort to escape anxiety, or to deny it, or to refuse to face it, that makes it impossible for the self to become authentic. If in anxiety a man is aware of his totality, and the only way something can be known as a totality is to know what its final outcome is, then to know man, or the self, as a totality means to know death as its final outcome. If the self is a totality only as completed, and it is not completed until it has come to an end, i.e., has died, then it is only by recognizing that the self is a being-unto-death that the self can be properly seen as a totality, and anxiety be faced. Yet to face death is to confront the possibility of the non-Being of the self, and that is something "they" do not want to face. "They" know "man must die," but only as a general statement about the ultimate fate of the race. Really to face death means to face it as the final possibility of the self as it stands alone, shorn of all other relationships. Each self must do its own dying by itself; "they" cannot do the dying for the self. Only when one faces the fact that he as an individual must die, only when he realizes that his own-most potential is being-to-death, will he understand that he cannot be himself by losing himself among "them." The realization of his death as an individual, alone, confronts the self with a moment of self-transparency: he sees himself as finite, and is faced with the choice of accepting that fact, and thus acknowledging himself as he truly is, or forgetting that fact by reimmersing himself in "them," in forgetfulness of his true self.

This self-transparency of the self to itself in confronting death also actualizes the true function of the self, i.e, its openness to Being. When it opens itself to its own Being as Being-unto-death, it achieves its proper stance of openness to Being, and has thus made the decision for authenticity. Transparency of the self to itself as Being-unto-death thus provides the point of decision for the self whereby it may decide to be what it is, and thus abandon "them" in whose clutches the self had lost itself as openness to Being because of its numbing traffic with beings. Authenticity, then, means: the decision to be the self one is, i.e., self-unto-death, and in affirming that, the self achieves its openness to Being, and escapes its imprisonment in beings.

It is the voice of conscience that summons the individual to the task of achieving this authentic selfhood. The conscience is thus the voice of there-being, summoning the self, lost as a being among beings, to take up again its true stance in openness to Being, i.e., as the there of Being. And that voice, summoning inauthenticity to authenticity, brings with it the feeling of guilt at having failed to become what the self ought to have become. The conscience thus calls the self to choose to be what it is, and in this choice to achieve authenticity.

Such a choice, however, cannot be made once and for all. It is a decision that must be made ever and anew, each time the self is tempted to lose itself among beings, among the mass. The self must therefore, as we saw earlier, continually be achieved; it can rest on no once-for-all accomplishment. Put another way, this means that the Being-question must continually be asked, if the self is to remain authentic. That is, the self must continue to hold itself open to Being. And this, in turn, is achieved by the will to know, which in its turn is carried out by questioning. Therefore, the authentic self remains open to Being by raising again and again the question of Being, by willing in that way to know Being, and by thus allowing Being to come to light in itself. In this way, the self has retrieved itself as the potentiality for becoming the there of Being which it has always been as a self, but which it must continually achieve as its own potentiality. The self must therefore actualize its potentiality (future), which is its very nature (past), in the present moment (present).

But this is a startling discovery. If we have, in fact, described the nature of authentic being as the self achieves it, then it becomes apparent that the very essence of the whole movement is time: past, present, and future. If the Being of man consists in his openness to Being, which seeks in man the place where it can come to light, then the horizon within which Being occurs is time, since the very essence of the self is to realize in the present its own nature (its past) which is its potentiality (its future). But even more, it indicates that time itself is grounded in the structure of the self, so that the possibility of temporal existence, i.e., history, is itself grounded in the structure of the self. History is therefore possible not because of some objective, exterior course of events in which man somehow participates, but because man is in his essence temporal, historical, and therefore history as a whole is possible because history, or time, is the very essence of the self.[5] Of the three dimensions of time, however, the future retains priority, since the self as the there of Being always has its task ahead of it. It is always coming to itself when it realizes its potential as the there of Being. Authentic selfhood must therefore be oriented to the future rather than the past.

In this way, in rather broad outline, Heidegger carries out his phenomenological analysis of man as a first step in asking the Being-question. This analysis occurs for the most part in Heidegger's first major work, *Being and Time*. But clearly, only preliminary work has been done. The question of Being, in a sense, still waits to be asked. As Heidegger develops his thought, he turns more and more from an analysis of man as the one who responds to Being, to the question about Being to which man responds. It is a shift in emphasis if not in substance, and we must now see what developments that shift brings in its wake.

3

Martin Heidegger — II

DURING THE FIRST PART of Heidegger's philosophical career, his approach to the question of Being centered on an analysis of the Being of man. His later writings have put more emphasis on Being itself. The first period put the emphasis on There-being (*Dasein*) as the place where Being comes to light. The second period puts more emphasis on the Being for which man functions as the "there." Heidegger turns more and more to a description of the primacy of Being over its "there," and to the place language plays in the coming to light of Being. If the first period could be characterized as "anthropological," the second could be termed "linguistic." It was the first period, as we shall see, that most influenced Bultmann, and the second that most influences the new hermeneutic.

We may begin our inquiry by investigating what Heidegger takes to be the proper meaning of the word "truth."[1] In its normal and common usage, "truth" is the conformity of a conception to the object conceived. I conceive of a chair as having four legs; if the chair does in fact have four legs, my concept is a "true" one. It conforms to the object so conceived. In that case, truth is descriptive of a concept, nothing else. And yet, Heidegger points out, a basic question remains unanswered. How do we *know* that such a judgment, or concept, is true? For it to be verified, we must discover something about the object itself. Only if that is possible can we verify a concept as true. Therefore, this "dis-covering" of the object, this possibility that the object can reveal itself, is the presupposition of "truth." Heidegger likes to support this argument by pointing out that the Greek word for "truth," *alētheia*, is a compound of a root that means "hidden" (*leth-*), and the alpha privative. Therefore, the Greek word for "truth" preserves the insight that truth means "deprived of hiddenness," or "open."[2] Truth thus presumes an openness on the part of the object, which lets us determine whether or not our concepts concerning it are true. But more, truth presumes a place where that openness of the object can "come to light," as it were. The real locus of truth, therefore, would be an openness to the manifestation, or "dis-covering" of an object that would let the object show itself for what it is. But this "openness" is precisely what man is. Man is the one who dis-covers objects, who lets them manifest themselves for what they are. Apart from man, therefore, there is no truth. To be sure, the objects themselves do not depend on man for their existence, but they cannot manifest themselves without a place where that can occur, and such a place is man.

If all of this sounds somewhat familiar, there is good reason. Much of what we have just said about truth can also be said of Being. Just as man is the "there" of Being, so man is the locus of truth. If Being is that by which beings are manifest, and if truth is the process of non-concealment, then Being and truth are closely related. If that is the case, furthermore, then we already begin to see the direction in which Heidegger's thinking about Being is going to move.

More needs to be said about truth, however. If man is the "locus" of truth, and there is therefore no truth apart from man, it is also true that man does not originate truth. In fact, if we carry our analysis a step farther, we will be forced to relocate the locus of truth. Before anything can be manifested to and by man, it must have within itself the capability of such "manifestation." Man will then simply respond to the "opening" of the being he conceives. If man's response to this opening is essential for truth, it is still a response to the "initiative" of—let us use the word—Being. Thus, the priority lies with truth, or, more precisely, with Being, which will become, for Heidegger, the coming-to-pass of truth in beings.[3]

Another consequence must be drawn from this understanding of truth. If truth is non-concealment, then non-truth would be concealment. And that is the case. The puzzling fact, is, in turn, that the two go hand in hand. In fact, if truth is non-conceal-ment, then there must be a prior concealment from which emergence may occur. If that concealment is non-truth, then non-truth would be the source of truth—or non-Being the source of Being! We run up against a problem here which pervades the thinking of the later Heidegger: the fact that Being both reveals and conceals itself. It reveals itself in beings, he will argue, but when beings come to light, Being withdraws itself into those beings. This, too, lies at the beginning of the path his thought follows, if we recall the definition of man as "finite transcen-dence." Man can transcend himself, and does, when he is open to the manifestation of beings, which is truth, yet as finite, he is not capable of being completely open to all things. Here the cause of concealment would lie in man. Could it be possible, however, that since man is the there of Being, that such con-cealment could be the very withdrawal of Being itself from man? But again, for that to happen, Being would have to take the initiative. And then to explain any truth at all, any non-con-cealment of Being, we would have to assume that Being gives itself at some points, and withdraws itself at others. What are those points? And how does man respond to that revealing, and to that concealing? These are the questions to which we must now turn our attention, in an effort to discern the contours of Heidegger's thought about Being, and of man's response to Being in language.

There can be little question, as we have already indicated, that for the "later" Heidegger, Being more and more assumes primacy over man. We had seen earlier that there-being (man) was necessary for Being, if Being were to emerge as itself, some-thing which, from another perspective, means that there-being exists for Being, so that Being may emerge. And in fact this is what Being does. When man discerns the ontological difference (between beings and Being) it is because Being bestows itself upon man. It is Being, therefore, that holds the initiative, that bestows itself upon man, that summons man to his task of thinking Being.

If, then, Being gives itself to man, opens itself to man, calls to man, as it were, then it is clear that Being is not something static, but something active, something that "sends itself" to man. This "sending" Heidegger calls *Geschick*, which, in addition to containing the root meaning of "send" is also the word for "fate." Thus Being, opening itself to man, holding the initiative, summoning man to respond to its self-emitting, is man's fate. It is Being that determines when and where it opens itself to man, and thus determines when and how man may respond to it. Since man's task is to respond to Being, Being leads him on, determines him, becomes, and is, his fate. But the self-emitting, occurring time and again, differently at different points, is then also constitutive of history, for history is simply the way man responds to his fate, Being, when it opens itself in a particular way. Thus it is this self-emitting by Being, by which it opens itself to man, which constitutes the process of history. But conversely, it is also true that Being is profoundly historical, revealing itself ever anew at different times. Being, as the self-opening of itself for man, as this creator of illumination, can also be characterized as an opening in the sense of an opening, or clearing, in the woods, which allows light to shine into the forest. In that way, Being "clears" itself by opening itself, sending itself to illumine men.

All of this means that if Being holds the initiative, man must be "docile" toward this Being, if he is to benefit from Being's self-emitting. Such docility takes place in thought. We may recall that we noted earlier there can be no Being apart from man. That means Being, in a sense, requires man to think it, if its openness is to be realized. Indeed, Heidegger seems to say, thought occurs simply as a response to Being, so that apart from the initiative of Being, there would be no thought. That again would mean that thought is essentially passive. Indeed, unless it is passive, it cannot be truly thought in the sense of a response to Being. Thought that is not passive seeks to grasp Being, to force it into some preconceived categories. This "active" thought Heidegger sees manifested in the attempt of a subject to master an object by forcing it into prior concepts, and then deciding how and where those concepts may legitimately be used. For that reason, the idea of knowledge as predicated on the "subject-object split" (i.e., man must observe something impartially in order to know something about it) and the idea of "objective" thought (i.e., thought which must pass certain tests, perhaps empirical verification, before it is accorded validity) are reckoned by Heidegger to be the chief reason why the self-opening of Being is ignored. That is also why Western philosophy, initiated by the insight into the self-opening nature of Being (e.g., truth as *a-lētheia* in Greek: "uncoveredness"), has since ignored Being by seeking to order and structure beings. Rather, the attitude of the thinker must be one of openness, of docility, of readiness to accept Being's self-opening. Thought must acknowledge the opening of Being as a gift, so that the most appropriate analogy of the way thought (*Denken*) is to be carried on is in the form of thanks (*Danken*).

We saw earlier, however, that Being is profoundly historical, that it opens itself repeatedly, and thus, operating as man's fate (*Geschick*), is itself the process of history (*Geschichte*). If thought, then, is to remain docile to Being, is to accept the initiative of Being, then it must follow that thought, too, is profoundly historical. Thought will be appropriate only as the response to the self-opening of Being. When Being in its richness opens itself in another way, a new form of thought will be demanded. For that reason, there can be no "absolute truths" of thought; when Being opens itself anew, only thought responsive to that new opening will be appropriate. Only faith, not thought, can claim such certainty, says Heidegger, and faith is outside the realm of philosophy.

As a further consequence, it follows that one cannot *refute* a thinker of the past. One can only ask about the opening of Being to which he meant to be responsive. But does that mean that thought is completely relative? No, since thought is always response to Being that opens itself. Thus, the unity and validity of thought rests in Being itself, which calls forth thought appropriate to its own self-emitting. A further corollary of the historic nature of Being would be the fact that truth, also, as the openness of Being, is historical.

Man's task, therefore, is to remain open for the self-opening of Being, to respond to it in the docility of thought, and thus transform Being, which opens itself to him, into history. The task is clear enough, and if Being initiates thought, it ought to be easy enough. Why, then, the decadence of thinking, as illustrated in the history of Western philosophy, and its decline into metaphysics? Why the confusion about recognizing the self-opening of Being? That problem has played a major part in Heidegger's thinking, and it has received an answer in several different ways. At times, the answer seems to lie in the fact that there-being, as finite, does not have the capacity to respond to an openness that goes beyond it. Again, the answer seems to lie in the fact that, paradoxically, Being withdraws itself into the beings which it makes manifest, and thus, in the very process of manifestation, hides itself. Again, if Being is worthy of thought, indeed demands thought, then it is also worthy of questioning, or, in different words, is eminently questionable, and as such is then capable of withholding itself from improper questioning. At other times, it appears that the reason for the unattainability of Being in its total clarity is the fact that Being itself, as finite, can only reveal itself in a finite way, i.e., in part. It is thus always limited by continuing concealment. But whatever the answer, there lies in Being not only self-opening, but self-concealing as well. There is some primal negativity within Being itself. But if man is to respond to Being, then he must respond to the negativity as well. By accepting Being in its negativity, and that means accepting the negativity of there-being as well, i.e., death, man responds to Being *as it opens itself up* in both its positive and negative aspects, and thus man, docile to Being, achieves authenticity.

But what then do we make of man's unwillingness to be docile to Being, his "forgetting of Being" which lies at the heart of the decadence of modern thought, with its attempt to control Being through the use of concepts and "objective thinking"? If it could be attributed to the inauthenticity of there-being, can it not also be attributed to the self-concealing of Being, i.e., its negativity? Indeed, could not the very inauthenticity of there-being be laid to the same source? However those questions are to be answered, it appears more and more that for Heidegger, the "forgottenness of Being" is due not so much to man's forgetting as it is due to Being itself. Surely, it is so in part at least because of the historical nature of Being: in disclosing itself to a given epoch in history, it also inevitably concealed itself as well. Full truth is granted to no historical period. Granted therefore the essentially finite character of Being's self-opening in history, thought, to be docile to Being, must be open to the negativity as well as the positivity of Being. In the last analysis, this forgottenness of Being, due to the negativity of Being, is due not to a lack in Being, but to the very richness of Being, because of which it cannot open itself fully at any one time. If that be so, then it would also follow that man cannot fully respond to the richness that is revealed; that there is more to be seen in man's response to the self-opening of Being than even they were aware who responded. It ought to be possible, then, by considering the response of a given thinker, to find more of the openness of Being in the thinker's response than that thinker himself was aware of when he formulated that response. And if that is so, then we ought to be able to retrieve something more of that openness than the thinker himself thought was to be had. But what is the nature of the thinker's response, that should make such a retrieving possible? To answer that question, we must consider the nature and function of language, as Heidegger understands it.

We enter, at this juncture, what is perhaps the most obscure, and most important, area of Heidegger's more recent thought. More and more in recent years, Heidegger has turned to a kind of oracular utterance, and a kind of esoteric philosophizing, which does not lead to the production of philosophical essays in the normal sense of the term. As a result, his more recent work is open to a variety of interpretations, and is capable of no adequate summary. We shall have to content ourselves here with a brief summary of what appear to us the more salient points for our present purposes.

Heidegger argues that the usual view of language, that it is the outward expression of man's inner emotional and intellectual disposition, or that words are signs of man's inward reaction to the objects he encounters, is totally insufficient to account for language. In fact, such a view of language is the result of man's forgottenness of Being, of the effect of his inauthenticity upon his view of language. To see the origin of language, we must recall our discussion about the priority of Being over its there (i.e., man as there-being), and man's necessary response. It is precisely this response which is the origin of language. Thus, language owes its existence not to man, but to Being, which summons language forth. Language therefore is the response to Being, it is the act of being-open-to Being, of letting-be-manifest in response to the call of Being. Language is, as it were, the answering hail to the hail of Being as it opens itself to man.

But what is there in Being that makes language the only appropriate response? Answer: Being itself is essentially nameable, and thus must eventuate in "naming," i.e., in language. Heidegger analyzes the German word for the act of using language, *Sagen* (speaking). This word has the basic meaning, he argues, of "letting appear," "showing," "causing to be seen." Yet that is precisely what Being is. Therefore at the heart of Being lies *Sage*, i.e., the root that makes "saying" (*Sagen*) possible. And since, as we saw earlier, Being needs man for its expression, it follows that this *Sage* needs its completion in language. Therefore language is man's response to the essential nature of Being which seeks to come to itself through expression in human language. Similarly, Heidegger can speak of language as the response to the "silent tolling of Being."[4] Language is therefore not the arbitrary creation of men, as some philosophers of language have asserted. Rather, language is the response forced upon man by the very nature of Being as it opens itself to man. For that reason, also, Heidegger can say that "language speaks" in man, meaning that Being (*Sage*) uses man in its drive to openness through language (*Sagen*). For Heidegger, therefore, language uses man, creates man to be what he is, so that Being may come to expression in man. Language is the place where Being may dwell, may find rest from its drive to come to expression in man. Language is thus the "house of Being."

Since, however, man in his inauthenticity is not docile to Being, and turns true language (*Rede*) into mere prolixity (*Gerede*), everyday language is a distortion of its original nature and intention. Language in its authenticity has the function simply of letting Being be, of allowing Being to come to expression, and of guarding Being from loss and distortion. Through language, Being seeks to let things be what they are, seeks to open beings to man, who is the "there," the place where that openness occurs. But if language is the response to the call of Being, then, conversely, language is man's access to Being. It is in language that Being achieves the openness toward which it drives. That means, in turn, that authentic language preserves Being, and makes it accessible. But who are the ones who perform this function? Who records the "event of Being"?

Foundational thinkers, for one. They are the ones who hear the silent toll of Being, and respond by allowing it to form language through them. In the words of foundational thinkers, then, there is the chance to find authentic language in the midst of prolixity. But there is another group to whom we must look for the language of Being, a group to whom Heidegger gives particular attention. They are the poets.

The reason for the preeminence of poets in the task of language lies, in part at least, in the fact that Heidegger's definition of poet is so close to his concept of true language. Poetizing is, in essence, the response of the poet, in the form of words, to the address he receives from Being. Thus the true poet does not compose, he fulfills his response to the call of Being. And if it is true that man must listen to Being, if he is to speak at all, then the poet is man functioning in language as man ought to function. That is, the poet is the one who has the primal experience: that the word allows a thing to "be," and to be present. It is the poet who allows Being to function as itself in words, i.e., as opening up a thing so that it may be what it is. This is also, Heidegger affirms, the purpose of all art, which seeks to gather the luminosity shed by Being, and responds to it in such a way that Being may shine forth. That would also mean, and for Heidegger it does, that all art is in essence a kind of poetry, a response to the hail of Being. In the poet, then, the address of Being is heard, and the response is shaped in words, in language.

But language, however aptly used, still bears within itself its own finitude, preventing it from responding fully to the fullness of Being's address. For that reason, there is more to the advent of Being than appears in the words spoken. For Heidegger, all language contains within itself the wealth of the event of Being that must, because of the sheer overpowering wealth of Being, remain unsaid and unexpressed. The true fullness of a poem or of a work of art, lies, therefore, in the unspoken or unexpressed that remains concealed in what is spoken or expressed. Therefore, not only can language not exhaust the riches of the event of Being, the language that does result is as important for what it is unable to say as for what it does say. And that, of course, has important consequences for one who approaches a text as interpreter. We shall consider those consequences in a moment.

There is, as we have seen, the most intimate kind of relationship between Being and language in the thought of Heidegger. If, as we have seen, Being is the process of coming to light, of manifestation, then language also shares in this lighting-process. Indeed, for Heidegger, apart from the word, the name, of a thing, there is only undifferentiated darkness. Therefore, in a sense, Being needs the word to "be," just as the word needs Being to call it forth. "The Being of everything that is," says Heidegger, "lives in the word. For that reason it is valid to say: Language is the house of Being."[5] And if man is man by reason of the fact that he can use language, or perhaps better, language can come to being in him, then the proper place for man as man to live is in this house of Being. Furthermore, if, as we have seen, Being discloses itself in a historical way, and the vehicle through which Being does disclose itself is language, then language is also man's fate, as the expression of the Being which is his fate. The language at a man's disposal, which he did not choose, and which he does not originate, determines for him the angle of vision he will have for the luminosity of Being which is opened up in that language. A man is therefore what he speaks, or perhaps more accurately, for Heidegger, a man is what Being discloses through him in language. Man, therefore, to be truly man, must respond to the call of Being in docility toward Being in the form of allowing it to shape his thought and his language. Man is authentic, then, to the extent that he allows himself to be the place (the "there") where Being as light, as luminosity, may occur. He is authentic to the extent that he himself therefore becomes a part of the process whereby Being, as luminosity, allows beings to stand forth out of the undifferentiated darkness of non-Being and to be what in fact they are, to emerge into the light of their own Being-what-they-are. For this allowing beings to Be, man is therefore a necessary part of the process; for such beings come to Be, come to light, in the *words* that allow the light of Being to illumine them, again from the darkness of undifferentiation. Until a thing is "named," i.e., has a word for itself, it cannot be understood or considered for what it itself is. So long as it remains unnamed, it cannot be singled out from its background. Until an "oak" is named, i.e., until a word identifies its uniqueness, it is just another tree in the (darkness of the) forest.

Man is thus entrusted with the task of being the locus ("there-being") where Being-as-the-light-of-beings-through-language may shine forth. In a way, Being is thus under man's care. Man is, in Heidegger's picturesque language, the "neighbor of Being," he is the "shepherd of Being," constantly charged with the task of responding to Being, lest darkness descend, and Being-as-light be lost.

The key, then, seems to lie in man's achieving authenticity, in becoming a part of this process of the truth of Being as emergence into light. To do this man must "think Being." But how is that to be done? The answer: by questioning. Being, it will be recalled, is compelled to reveal itself in beings (as against revealing itself apart from beings), and, because of Being's immense richness, it cannot reveal itself completely. It is also concealed, as well as revealed, in beings. Being thus gives itself in a questionable way, as it were, never clearly and completely. If man is to respond to that Being, he must do it then by questioning, by continually raising the question of Being. If the question is never finally answered—and it cannot be, so long as the event of Being is historical, and history continues—it can nevertheless be refined, so that in each instance Being is forced to disclose more of itself than before. Such repeated questioning is a circular process, but only in that way, only by such questioning and requestioning, can man remain docile to Being. In this ever-repeated structure of question, answer, and further question, we meet again the "hermeneutical circle," in which each answer allows man to refine his question in the light of his answer, so that the question may probe ever more deeply into the hidden riches of Being.

We have also seen that authenticity involves responding to the self-opening, the event of Being, in appropriate language. That would mean that part of the data to be questioned would consist in the kind of response made in the past to the advent of Being. In that way, Being *comes* to man from the words of the *past event* of Being, and requires by its coming that it *be expressed* again, as response to its coming, in language. Here again, however, we recognize the essentially historical structure of Being, and of man in his response to it: it comes (future) from past expression (past) to be expressed now (present). Thus, the structure of Being corresponds to the historical structure of the self which we discovered earlier. Further, it is precisely this historical structure which is represented by meditation upon the linguistic response to the event of Being, i.e., studying the (historical) words of some foundational thinker or some poet. One must open himself to Being as it comes to him (future) from these words (past) so that he may express it anew (present). By such dialogue with the past, we allow Being to come once more into words.

Yet we are not in the same place, historically, as those who first uttered those words. History—the eventful self-opening of Being —has continued, and we stand in a different light, under a different "fate," from the author of those words. We are therefore in a position to see something more of the riches of the event of Being to which those words responded. In fact, we must see something other than simply what the author intended, or at least thought he intended, if we are to respond adequately to the Being that seeks to open itself to us *now* in that text. To do any less would be to violate the historical character of Being and of the self. Thus, to achieve authenticity as adequate response to Being, one must "retrieve" the origins of man's response to the self-opening of Being, and in this way allow the origin (past) to come to him (future) now (present). But that means more than mere repetition; it means learning more from such origins than was apparent at the time of those origins. It means purifying them from the dross that has collected about them, as the original words became common parlance, and their original luminosity was thus tarnished, or lost altogether.

To advance to the openness of Being, we must now discern something of the hidden riches latent in that original response. That means we *must* find more than the "original intention" of the text! "Retrieve" means no more nor less than the attempt to respond to the riches of the event of Being which the author himself did not, indeed could not, express. Thus, the only genuine retrieve means that the text must be understood differently than the author understood it. To do less is to be less than open to Being. It is the *unsaid* in a text, forced to remain unsaid because the event of Being is historical, finite, and thus limited, which is the true object of such retrieve, for only in this can the event of Being come to us again for new expression in our language. Thus, thought formed in response to later events (self-disclosures) of Being, and thus enriched by such further responses, can liberate more of the event of Being that is expressed in earlier language than could the one who originally uttered those words! In this way, Being continually summons forth, and renews language, and thereby makes possible the retrieve of ever more light from earlier language. Thus the study of the past reveals to us more of the true *coming* of Being, i.e., of the future.[6]

Retrieve is therefore, in a sense, a key conclusion of Heidegger's thought, for by it the (inevitable) fallenness of Being, and therefore of language, may be overcome, and the original freshness of the event of Being recovered, by heeding the event of Being as it expresses itself to us now through the response (the language) to its advent in the past (text). And precisely this recovering, this retrieve, this allowing Being to come to light through language, this "interpretation" of the event of Being in language, is what is meant by "hermeneutics." It is man's task, through docility to the event of Being in contemporary history, as well as through dialogue with the linguistic crystallization of the response to such events in the past, to allow Being to come to language through himself, thus taking his authentic place within the total process of the self-opening of Being.

Such is the kind of thought, then, in which the new hermeneutic is anchored, and in terms of which it seeks to carry out its theological task. Since, as we noted earlier, we are not primarily interested in Heidegger's thought as such, but only as part of the background necessary to understand the new hermeneutic, we shall not attempt a critique, or evaluation, of his thought. Such evaluations are continually being made, both from theological and philosophical perspectives, and there is no point in trying to summarize them here.[7] We shall turn, rather, to an examination of the way in which Rudolf Bultmann sought to make use of some of the insights of Heidegger's thinking in his, Bultmann's, attempt to frame the gospel message in terms understandable to modern man.

4

Rudolf Bultmann

THE IMPORTANCE of the work of Rudolf Bultmann for current theological thinking can scarcely be overestimated. His own lifetime has spanned the period from the height of "liberal" theology (he was born in 1884), through the period of "neo-orthodoxy," in which he played a prominent part, and on into the present time of "new directions." He spent almost his entire career at the University of Marburg, where he assumed the chair of New Testament in 1921 and held it until he retired in 1950. During that period he was a leading figure in the rise of form criticism; in the development of "existential" theology and interpretation; in the formation and activity of the "Confessing Church," a group that resisted the National Socialist aims for the Lutheran Church in Germany; and in the attempt to demythologize the New Testament. Many of the chairs of New Testament in the leading German universities are currently held by men who studied under him, and his influence shows itself in the fact that one of his primary concerns, interpreting the New Testament, has now become a major theme in a good deal of contemporary theology. For that reason, if for no other, any attempt to understand the new hermeneutic, which has such interpretation as its central concern, will of necessity have to take Bultmann's thought into account.

There is another reason why we must consider his thought, however. If, as we have said, the roots of the new hermeneutic lie in the kind of thinking that we see in the philosophical endeavors of Heidegger, it is also true that part of those roots, at least, draw on Heidegger through the way in which Bultmann made use of Heidegger's categories. That is to say, while "Heidegger—II" has something of a direct influence, or line of similarity, with the kind of matters with which the new hermeneutic concerns itself, part at least of the problems of the new hermeneutic have been inherited from Bultmann, and his attempt to make Heideggerian categories, more particularly those of "Heidegger—I," fruitful for theological thinking and New Testament interpretation. We must attempt to see, in this chapter, the way in which Bultmann draws on Heideggerian formulations in an attempt to solve the theological problem of interpretation, and the kind of problems which Bultmann, in the eyes of his followers, had not been able to deal with in an entirely satisfactory manner.

What we will attempt, therefore, is by no means a discussion of the whole of Bultmann's thought. Most of his major works are now available in English, and many good studies have been written about him.[1] Rather, we want to look at those points in Bultmann's thought which will help indicate something of the nature and background of the problems with which the new hermeneutic deals. It is difficult, however, to discuss only part of Bultmann's thought, since all parts interlock, and to pick up any one idea is like pulling a loose thread in a knitted garment: sooner or later, you are involved with the whole matter. This is also true with respect to the development of Bultmann's thought. In an almost unique way, his position is consistent through his academic lifetime. The vocabulary may occasionally change—the word "demythologizing" is of later coinage, although the attempt to reinterpret myth occupies Bultmann almost from the beginning of his published writings—but the basic problem, that of interpreting New Testament thought into categories understandable to the twentieth century, remains the same. In a sense, that fact simplifies our task, by removing the necessity of differentiating early and later stages of development. It also gives us something of a free hand in deciding where we want to begin our consideration of his thinking. Perhaps the best place, for our purposes, would be with his thought concerning the task of interpreting the New Testament, so let us begin there.

Any consideration of ancient documents and the attempt to understand them involves one immediately in some form of historical research, if the understanding of those documents is in any way to be protected from purely arbitrary interpretation. Over the past century or so, a method has been evolving, and has won general consent, for approaching such historical problems. This "historical method" works on the basis of certain presuppositions, which anyone dealing in the interpretation of ancient texts must observe if the results of his investigations are to be credible to twentieth-century man. One of those presuppositions, Bultmann argues, is that history is a closed, causal continuum. That is to say, history is seen as a unity in the sense that cause and effect are operative in it, not to the exclusion of free decision, of course, but even a free decision is the cause of what follows, and is itself made in the light of given conditions. This unity is presumed to be complete in itself in the sense that the modern historian also assumes that sufficient cause for all historic events can be found within history. The modern secular historian no longer looks for (possible) supernatural causes to explain a historical course of events. This historical method, Bultmann argues, is the absolute presupposition for any serious work with historical materials, including the New Testament.[2] That means, in turn, that any attempt to make the New Testament understandable to modern man will have to understand history in that way. Neither God nor his acts can any longer be reckoned with as a part of the causal nexus of historical events. To view the New Testament that way would mean the elimination from serious consideration of the miraculous as an event whose cause did not lie within history, a consequence Bultmann is able to contemplate with equanimity.

In this regard, Bultmann argues, modern man differs from the persons who lived at the time the New Testament was being written. Those writers, as children of their time, did apparently regard God, or his activity, as a possible link in the chain of historical events. Such thinking Bultmann characterizes as "mythological." In his original essay on demythologizing, Bultmann defined such "myth" as "the use of imagery to express the other worldly in terms of this world and the divine in terms of human life, the other side in terms of this side." In later writings, however, he worked with a definition that designated as mythological any thought in which God was reckoned as part of the causal nexus of events, in which God "interfered" with, or became a direct causal link within, the course of nature or history or the inner life of man.[3] For all practical purposes, "myth" designates the same kind of event that is usually referred to by the use of the word "miracle," where that word is used to refer to some act of God.

It is clear, then, that if the New Testament is to be made comprehensible to modern man, such "myths" must be got rid of. Yet it is also apparent that there is more to myth than just its imagery. In fact, Bultmann argues, myths are designed really to express man's understanding of himself in relation to his world. When myths speak of gods and demons, they give expression to man's realization that he is not master of his world and of his own life, that he is surrounded, rather, by mystery. Myths express an understanding of human existence. The difficulty is that sooner or later, the imagery tends to be taken literally, so that the words that once expressed a genuine insight into the nature of human existence become commonplace assertions about the objective structure of reality. When that happens, the original intention of the myth is totally obscured.

The task of interpretation, therefore, is to recover this original intention of the mythical formulations and express it in terms that make sense to modern man, who can no longer share the view of the universe which these formulations reflect. "Demythologizing" therefore means, not to pluck out and eliminate the myths, but rather to determine what understanding of existence the ancient writers and thinkers sought to express by means of mythical imagery. Thus, the mythical expression "heaven," understood as a locality "up there," expresses the idea that God is not bound by this world; the idea of Satan and his minions expresses the experience that men are carried away by evil passions, and are no longer in control of themselves; Paul's "cosmic powers" indicate that man is enslaved to powers for whose dominion he is nevertheless himself responsible. In short, myths point to man's experience that he is not his own master, that he experiences limitations he himself did not establish, and that forces are at work upon him over which he is unable to exercise control. They point to man's lack of security in the world. Bultmann has on occasion argued that in this way, demythologizing makes the same point as does the doctrine of justification by faith, with the one exception that in the case of demythologizing, the point is being made in the area of epistemology. Both justification by faith and demythologizing point to man's lack of security, whether it is based on good works, or on "objectifying knowledge," i.e., knowledge that man can use and apply for his own benefit and salvation. Both justification by faith and demythologizing, Bultmann argues, mean that "he who abandons every form of security shall find the true security. Man before God has always empty hands."[4]

It is one thing to discern the original intention of the myth; it is another thing to find a structure of ideas into which to translate that intention so that it makes sense to modern man. To tell such a man that he is not the master of his own situation will likely bring the rejoinder that although that may be true for the time being, given a little time it will no longer be true, with man's increasing control over his environment. How then is this insight into human existence contained in the New Testament myths to be put so that modern man takes it seriously? The answer would be found if it could be put in terms of an understanding of existence which every modern man shared, consciously or not, i.e., an understanding of human existence given with that existence itself. In that case, modern man would have to take it seriously, because it would speak in the very terms by which he understands his own existence in the modern world. But where is such an understanding of existence to be found, analyzed, and capable of use in this way? Bultmann believes that he has found it in the phenomenological analysis of human existence carried out by Martin Heidegger. This analysis can provide the means whereby those ancient insights, cast in mythical terms, can be stated with compelling force to modern man. It will remove from myth its false claim to impart information about "objective reality," about the way things are in a literal sense, and restore to myth its rightful purpose as an expression of what it is like to live as a man in the world.[5]

The interpreter's task, therefore, is to see through the historically conditioned mode of expression found in the New Testament text to the "fundamental idea" (Bultmann's words) that lies behind and motivates that (mythical) expression.[6] But how is it possible to cross that yawning, historical gulf of two millennia which stands between us and the New Testament world? What do we have in common with those men? Answer: our lives, as theirs, as indeed all lives, are, wittingly or unwittingly, "impelled by the question about God."[7] And that in turn is so because in the end, to raise questions about human existence as such is to raise the question about, to search for, God. That means that the concern of the New Testament writers is the concern of every man, but it also means that what they write is of significance for me, since we are both moved by the same basic questions. This is what gives urgency to the task of interpretation: to miss what they have to say may be to miss the answer to the question of life itself.

This also gives us the clue to the way in which these texts are to be approached. No text can be understood unless the proper questions are addressed to it. And no text will be understood unless one has some inkling of what the text is all about. One who is ignorant of law, and has no interest in it, will gain a good deal less from an ancient legal text than a lawyer with a burning interest in an ancient solution to his own problem. This latter person will be involved in the subject matter treated in the text, and will know what questions are to be raised, so that he will recognize it when they are answered. This "life-relationship" to the text, this "pre-understanding," is what makes it possible to understand a historical text. And that is, of course, precisely what gives to the New Testament its universal significance, since its subject matter is the question about God and the meaning of man's existence. And that is, as we have seen, the one question that all men share, consciously or not. Therefore, simply to be involved in life is pre-understanding enough to enable one to approach the New Testament.

All of that, finally, indicates the way a historical writing, in general, and the New Testament, in particular, are to be approached. We get nowhere in trying to understand such material if we approach it as a neutral non-participant. The objective (i.e., non-involved) viewpoint, cultivated by the natural scientists, will guarantee only that the historical material will *not* be understood. The "subject-object" schema has no validity here. What history requires is not "objective" knowledge, but subjective involvement in the same basic issues as those raised, and discussed, in the material being studied. This personal involvement in the historical material under consideration is the "fundamental presupposition" for understanding history, and that means that the most "objective" interpretation, i.e., that which best understands and transmits the meaning, of a historical text is the most "subjective," i.e., the one most involved in the matters with which the text is dealing.[8]

We have now seen the task: to demythologize, i.e., to express the understanding of existence which is contained in the New Testament and given expression in myths. We have found the conceptual scheme that will enable us to do this: the understanding of existence given with existence itself, which the phenomenological analysis of Heidegger makes available. We have discovered the way to approach these New Testament writings which are separated from us by the historical gulf of two thousand years: we must take seriously the question that impels all human life, the question about self and thus about

God; and by such involvement in the subject matter of the text we shall be able to understand the answers that are offered there. We must now examine the results of this whole enterprise, that is, look at the way Bultmann seeks to express the New Testament understanding of existence in demythologized form.

Bultmann accepts the existential discovery that man's self-hood is not a metaphysical entity, given with the being of man, and needing only the proper circumstances to unfold itself, like a flower from a bud. Rather, the human self must continually strive to form itself in its decisions. In short, Bultmann accepts as presupposition the Heideggerian analysis of the nature of the self as one that must constantly seek to achieve that selfhood which is in turn its own potentiality. That means each self can either gain or lose itself, at any time, in its existence. Further more, since the self is fundamentally a relationship to itself rather than a fixed set of potentialities, it functions on the basis of this self-relationship, which can be expressed as its own self-understanding. The self will react to its own possibilities in accordance with the way it understands itself. Now this self-understanding will not necessarily be conscious; it is not to be confused with a given state of self-conciousness. It is not what a person thinks he is, or even consciously thinks about himself. His self-understanding consists rather in those values and decisions which the self makes as a matter of course. It is the realm of the "self-understood," the area of those things which are so obvious to the self that they form the basis of all acts and evaluations, without themselves necessarily always being consciously or deliberately employed. But each encounter puts such a self-understanding to the test. If the "normal" reaction proves inadequate, the self-understanding is thrown into question, and will then become the subject of deliberate examination, and perhaps be changed in the light of the new situation. Thus selfhood consists in the decisions made (present) when the self in its understanding of itself (past) is confronted with the events that come to it (future).

The difficulty with man, as the Bible sees it, says Bultmann, is that man operates with a false understanding of himself and his existence. Because man is naturally anxious about the future, he seeks to ensure himself against it by taking control of himself, and, to the extent that he can, his environment, both human and non-human. Man seeks to impose the past, which is known, and to some extent thus under his control, on the future, which is unknown and hence beyond his control. In this way, he seeks to protect himself from anything shatteringly new, or threatening, in the future. But in this act of seeking to secure himself by means of the past, that past gains the upper hand. Man has understood himself in a way dictated by the past, and seeks to deal with himself as with any other object, securing it against a possibly threatening future.[9] In a sense, man seeks to save from (future) destruction the self he knows, and in doing that, he falls more and more victim to the dictates of the past in whose terms he seeks such self-salvation. But to do that means to close himself off from the future, and from those possibilities of selfhood creating decisions which alone allow him continually to affirm his selfhood, thus preserving it by ever creating it anew. To try to save the self in that way is thus clearly to lose it. Such attempts to secure the self from threatened destruction take the form of radical self-assertion, and that is what the New Testament means by the word "sin." It is not a quality inherent in man; otherwise responsibility for it could not be laid on man. Yet it is inevitable in that every man, living in the world, tends to understand himself and therefore secure himself in terms of the world and its past. Sinful man thus understands himself as one who can save himself, i.e., secure himself against the future, shaping his existence as he sees fit for his own benefit, and doing that, if necessary (and it regularly is), at the expense of other men. The more he tries to secure himself in this way, however, the more it becomes apparent that it cannot be done, and the only response open to him is more and more self-assertion, with the increasing anxiety this brings as the man faces the fact that he cannot in fact secure his own existence. It is a vicious circle, from which sinful man cannot escape. He is bound to the past which has given him a false self-understanding (i.e., an understanding of the self as one that can secure itself), and he cannot escape it, since everything he does is controlled by that very past which has made him what he is.

It is into this situation that God speaks his word in Christ. Now if this revelation by God of himself in Christ is to have any effect on man, it will have to be accomplished in a way that man, constituted as we have described him, can benefit from it. This revelation of God in Christ, therefore, Bultmann argues, will not consist in some alteration of metaphysical conditions, whereby man is altered in some "objective" way by such "objective facts" of salvation. By "objective facts" of salvation, Bultmann means historic events which by the sheer fact that they happened, somehow change man's nature, or ensure, or even affect, his salvation. Unless the meaning of such events is appropriated existentially by man, i.e., put into practice in his life, Bultmann cannot conceive how they could influence man. To think that a past event, unknown to modern man, could nevertheless somehow decisively affect him, is for Bultmann nothing other than to think mythologically. The cross and resurrection as "saving events" therefore do not by themselves affect man one way or the other; to be effective, in Bultmann's view, their meaning must be appropriated into a man's life.[10]

Nor does the revelation of God in Christ consist in the impartation of knowledge about God, which a man could appropriate in the same way he appropriates any other truth "about" some object. Such knowledge of God is impossible, argues Bultmann, because any "objective" statement about God would be a statement in which the relationship between God and human existence would be ignored. That is impossible, since for Bultmann, every statement about God is also a statement about man, because we can know God only in his relationship to us. Hence, any statement about God that fails to take that relationship into account is the statement of an "observer," i.e., "objective" in the sense of non-participatory, and thus outside the realm of faith. That kind of "statement about" God is not to be taken seriously. Man knows God only in faith, and if, as Bultmann believes, faith is an existential relationship to God, any statement about God made outside the realm of faith, and thus of commitment, will *eo ipso* be false. Therefore, for Bultmann, any "objective" knowledge of, or statements about, God are impossible. "God-talk" for Bultmann is confessional, or it is false. God's word to man, His revelation, cannot therefore take the form of imparting "knowledge about" God.[11]

Rather, God's word in Christ confronts man with an event that forces him to call his self-understanding into question, and that puts man in a new situation with regard to the way he views his past and his future. The meaning of Christ's death on the cross is the death of man's values. If the crucified Christ is proclaimed as Lord, then it means that God has judged the world and its "desires and strivings and standards of value."[12] The death of Jesus thus represents the death of man to his old world, to his past and therefore to his old self-understanding. By renouncing such attempts to secure his own self, by renouncing all power and boasting, man confronts the death of his very self. Just as is the case with the Kingdom of God itself, death seen in the cross of Christ means "the end of earthly human existence as we know it."[13]

Man, in short, confronted with the cross, can decide to accept this judgment on his own self-understanding, and see himself now as one dependent on God, not himself. Such a decision is faith. Faith therefore represents the decision to see in whatever happens to a man, God's act for him. Faith thus provides the light by which man can see, *within* the normal course of events, God's activity on his behalf. Man is thus freed from his false understanding of himself which bound him to his past, and is therefore now open for the future. He is now, in the light of Christ's cross, free from death, but from a death seen, not as a natural power—all men must die physically—but in its meaning as something that cuts off all future. The self is now free to face the future as a gift of God. It is also free from the necessity of securing itself at the expense of others. It can allow others to live, it can act in love. And such self-surrender in love means death is in fact overcome. All of this means, of course, that man is now free from the world, its cares and anxieties, which had forced upon him a false understanding of himself.

Bultmann appears here to be drawing on a particular insight of Heidegger. We saw that, for Heidegger, man's true Being, as finite, is Being-unto-death. That means that for Heidegger the ultimate goal of man's selfhood is to give up the self, in death. If that is the true goal of the self, is there any point where the goal of the self could be reached this side of death? Yes, argues Bultmann, if we could locate the point at which the self has died to itself, without the man having suffered physical death. But that would be the same as living in resurrection; i.e., having died to its self, the self can live freed of it. That furnishes the key to understanding the cross and resurrection of Jesus. Jesus' death means that Jesus was willing to give up the affirmation of his selfhood even to the point of sacrifice on the cross; his resurrection means we confess he did this *for us*. If we, then, in faith that Jesus died for us, now live as a result in the kind of self-abandonment shown in Jesus' cross, we now live beyond death. That is, we, in faith, have died to our old self, which was tied to the sin and guilt of our past, and can now live as new men, beyond death. Such life would be "eschatological" in the Biblical intention of that term, i.e., living beyond the natural history of the self. "Eschatological existence" for Bultmann thus means to live freed from the past (history) and open to the future, having abandoned all self-security and self-assertion. That in turn is made possible by accepting the word of grace spoken to us in Jesus which tells us that such self-justification is unnecessary in the light of God's acceptance of us.

Christ's death upon the cross is therefore the event that enables the self to free itself from a false self-understanding based on the world, and to open itself to a new self-understanding, i.e., as a child of God. Death on the cross brings about the decision of faith, and thus the possibility of true selfhood open to the future.

Such a decision of faith, such a new self-understanding, will be constantly challenged, however, in every situation in which it finds itself. Thus, the decision for faith must be made again and again. God's word can still be drowned by the comforting murmur of everydayness, and the life of faith needs to be decided forever and anew. It is for this reason that the proclamation of Jesus' cross is so essential. It is this proclamation which calls ever and again for the decision of faith, which enables man to remain free from the world and its past and open for the future. It is proclamation, responded to in faith, which allows the new self-understanding to continue to operate.

Thus, the self, freed from the self-understanding given it by the world, can understand itself as a self open to the future, thus allowing it to achieve its true selfhood in decision; or put in more religious language, man is forgiven the sins of the past in the cross of Christ, and thus freed, he can face the future with faith that God is coming to him within the events of his world. Man comes in this way to know that he is not his own master. He abandons the false attempts to control his own destiny, and he gives himself into the hands of God, seeing God working for him in worldly events illumined by the light of faith.[14] Only by responding to God's self-revelation in Christ, therefore, can the self achieve authenticity as a self by truly facing its own potentiality (future) as the self that it is (past) in the decisions it is required to make (present). Only through the self-understanding of faith can the self be open to the future, as it must if it is to become truly a self.

This kind of restatement of the meaning and nature of the Christian faith can look quite radical from a number of angles, and of course the program of demythologizing was met with a storm of protest both in Germany and in other countries as well. It is not our purpose to review or evaluate those criticisms, just as it is not our purpose to give anything more than a mere sketch of Bultmann's position. We do want to indicate, however, some of the aspects of Bultmann's thought which seem to call for the kind of further development that is then attempted in the new hermeneutic. We want to see the roots in Bultmann of some of the problems with which the new hermeneutic feels compelled to deal.

Much has been written about the relationship between philosophy and theology in Bultmann's thought, and specifically about his use of Heidegger. Bultmann is quite clear in his own mind that he is simply using the conceptions worked out by the philosopher Heidegger to restate the basic insights into existence contained in the Christian faith. Time and again, Bultmann makes the point that every exegete and every theologian is involved in the use of philosophical concepts, either consciously or unconsciously. How much better, argues Bultmann, to be aware of one's philosophical presuppositions, even choose them with care, rather than have one's philosophical assumptions lead him, all unaware, into positions that are finally indefensible. It is not a question of whether or not to use terminology that has philosophical implications. All terminology has them. It is a question, rather, of finding terms from the "best" philosophy, from the "right" philosophy, i.e., the one best suited to making the Christian point. As to his "selling out" to Heidegger in terms of allowing Heidegger's analysis to pre-determine the results the Christian interpreter can come to, Bultmann rightly points out that Heidegger does nothing more than examine the basic structure of existence, i.e., inauthentic and authentic existence, with decision as the necessary transition from the former to the latter. Heidegger does not indicate the *content* of that decision. In a sense, what the philosopher deals with in the abstract (the structure of human existence), the theologian deals with in the concrete (how human existence is to be carried on). And, Bultmann points out, under Heidegger's terms, there is no chance ever to be free from one's past, for even the one deciding to be free from his past will still, as the self making that decision, inevitably be colored by that past. Only if the decision to be made comes to man from outside of himself can man truly make a decision to live unhampered by his past. The Christian faith alone, argues Bultmann, offers such a decision.[15]

A broader question poses itself in this respect, however, and it centers around the fact that Heidegger himself has gone well beyond the philosophical thinking represented in his earlier phase, of which Bultmann made use. One ought surely to explore the theological resources in Heidegger's thinking in its later stages if its very development implies the inadequacy of those earlier formulations. Can theology stick to a kind of philosophy which the philosopher himself has, if not repudiated, at least gone beyond? Therefore, the very philosophy that Bultmann chose as, in his judgment, the "right" one, all but compels those who take Bultmann seriously to go beyond him.

A second area around which much discussion has ranged is the question of the availability of knowledge, historical knowledge, about Jesus of Nazareth. Bultmann, convinced partly by his own discoveries of the nature of the sources for such knowledge, i.e., the Gospels, and partly by the theological excesses of the liberal "life of Jesus" movement, argued that such knowledge is unavailable, and rightly so. All we need to know about Jesus is the fact that he is the revealer.[16] That alone is enough to make us realize that we are not our own masters, and that our own quest for security is fruitless. Any further knowledge about Jesus as a person would simply contribute to our desire to achieve self-security apart from God. Indeed the very desire to possess such knowledge is an act of unfaith. It represents the desire to have our security located somewhere other than faith in God, who destroys all human security.[17]

But can the historical Jesus be so lightly dismissed? One distinction, at least, between the Christian faith and its competitors in the Hellenistic world rested in the fact that the Christians claimed their revelation to be grounded in historic reality. If that grounding is ignored, does not the Christian faith run the danger of becoming simply another exposition of some mythicophilosophical system that claims to purvey the timeless truths of the gods and man? Furthermore, Bultmann's own studies in the Gospels indicated the way in which the primitive church adapted Jesus' sayings to meet new circumstances as they arose. If *Jesus* is thus shown to be the foundation of the Christian faith, then is it not important to know, as clearly as possible, wherein the later adaptations differed from Jesus, so that we may judge the validity of those adaptations for our time, if for no other reason? Can the difficulty of this task of historical research be used as a reason not to undertake it? Such reasons, among others, seem to indicate the need continually to raise the question precisely about the historical Jesus, lest the Christian faith, loosed from its historic moorings, drift off to become yet another world view. Bultmann himself had fought hard and long to keep the Christian faith from becoming just such a world view, in terms of which it would be possible to make "objective statements" about God. It was precisely the need to keep the Christian faith from becoming merely another world view, however, which drove Bultmann's followers to reopen the question about the historical Jesus.

A third area of unfinished work concerns itself with Bultmann's program of demythologizing. It is apparent, in reading Bultmann, that he was never able really to divest himself completely of mythological terminology. Such phrases as "decisive act of God in Christ," "the redemptive action of God," "gift from God," "God . . . as a power which embraces and sustains [man] . . . ," "God steps in and acts," God "gives up Jesus to be crucified," make that rather clear.[18] To claim that such statements are not mythological, but analogical, as Bultmann does, is to confuse analogy and myth almost beyond possibility of distinction.[19] If the program of demythologizing is to be carried to completion, it is apparent that some method of explicating the Christian faith will have to be found which will enable one to speak of the insights of the Christian faith for man's existence without recourse to such mythological language. For those who take the proposal to demythologize the New Testament seriously, it appears that the task has yet to be completely accomplished.

Such problems, then, as the right philosophical conceptuality for expressing the Christian faith in a contemporary idiom, the relationship of the Jesus of history to Christian proclamation, and adequately carrying to completion the task of demythologizing the New Testament have been bequeathed by Bultmann to those who are impressed by his theological endeavor, and who seek as a result to carry it forward. It should cause no surprise, then, to see them recurring when we come to look at the new hermeneutic.

5

Language, Perception, and Reality

IN OUR DISCUSSION of the thought of Martin Heidegger, particularly with regard to its more recent developments, we noted that he has given his attention increasingly to the nature of language and its role in man's task of responding to Being. For him, as we saw, such a response takes the form of language, so that it is precisely this linguistic response which makes man what he is, namely, the place where Being comes to light. This importance of language for human nature, and for man's contact with his world and his fellowmen, has also impressed itself upon the proponents of the new hermeneutic, and it plays, as we shall see, a key role in their thinking as well. For them, too, man is defined as a linguistic being.

That language does in fact play a key role in human existence few would want to deny. Yet to affirm that language not only reflects but is also capable of altering and even creating reality seems so difficult to grasp, if not to be quite wrong altogether, that it is necessary to look at the whole question of the relationship between the way man operates within the world, and the way his perception of that world functions. To do this we want to consider briefly the nature of perception, and of perceptual activity, and then look at the place language occupies within such activity and the influence language seems to exert upon it. The new hermeneutic does not explicitly call upon this kind of evidence to support its assertions, but we will probably be in a somewhat better position to appreciate the key place they assign

to language if we are aware of the way psychological experiments
tend to point in similar directions. This is of course in no way
to affirm that data derived from experiments in perception
"prove" the validity of the theological insights represented in
the views of the new hermeneutic. All we wish to do is indicate
the kind of empirical data available that can demonstrate the
great importance of language for man and his contact with reality, so that the reader is not taken completely by surprise at
the assertion, made in the new hermeneutic, that language is
the key to understanding human nature, and the relationship
between man and God. We are not trying to demonstrate the
validity of the theological conclusions of the new hermeneutic.
We simply want to show that there is other evidence which
points to the importance of language for man and his traffic
with the world, and which is thus helpful for understanding a
theological position that has a similarly high evaluation of the
significance of language.

We must begin with a quite elementary assertion: our contact
with the world around us is mediated to us by means of sensory
perception. In this way we get the raw data on the basis of which
we then react to the world. There was a time when this process
was thought to take place upon an essentially passive man. Man
was, as it were, a blank tablet upon which the outside world
wrote its message by means of the five senses. Such a view has
been severely challenged, however, both philosophically and on
the basis of experimental data. It is apparent, for example, that
a person will tend to notice more readily those things in which
he is interested, or about which he knows something, or with
which he has pleasant associations. A father, mother, and child
walking down a street will perceive rather different things, even
though they face the same sensory stimuli. The mother is more
likely to notice the hat of another woman than is either the
man or the child, whereas the child will notice a toy store more
rapidly than either parent. Much of what we experience with
our senses is the direct result of what we "intend" to see. We
can "aim" our perception to the exclusion of much other sen-

sory stimuli, as in the case of a person reading intently, who will not "hear" sounds that another, not similarly absorbed, will "hear," even though both are subjected to sound waves of equal pitch and intensity. Much, therefore, that seems immediate in sense perception is quite arbitrary, and influenced by factors other than sensory organs or strength of stimuli.

This "selective" or "intentional" nature of perception can be demonstrated in the laboratory of the perceptual psychologist. For example, it can be shown, by means of tests for recognizing the presence of a musical tone, that a person is much more likely to detect its presence if he knows the tone whose presence he is to identify. If the person is expecting one tone, and receives another, he is less likely to detect the stimulus than would be the case were the expected tone to appear. The experiment naturally eliminates the possibility of chance detection, or of "hearing" an expected tone that was not actually present. An unexpected stimuli is thus measurably less likely to be detected than one that is expected.[1] Again, it has been demonstrated, for example, that motivation, or psychological need, can influence perception, as in the case of an experiment in which people with a "high affiliation need" were given glimpses of pictures of four familiar objects, one of which was a human face, and then asked which picture appeared brightest. More pictures of the human face were selected as brightest by those subjects with a high affiliation need than were so selected by a control group with a lower affiliation need. Needless to say, the illumination and exposure duration were quantitatively identical at all times, and yet that group which most needed other people "saw" human faces in a different way than others did.[2]

Other experiments have indicated the way in which "perception" varies, depending on differing circumstances. Thus, a person who looked at a physically curved line for a period of some minutes "observed" that the line became somewhat "straighter" with the passage of time, and a physically straight line, viewed after long exposure to a curved line, was "seen" to be curved in the opposite direction.[3] This is called "figural after-effect" and indicates the way in which perception is affected by the subject. Another experiment equipped the subject with a pair of prismatic lenses that reversed the image which normally appears upon the retina; i.e., through the glasses, the world looked "upside down." At first, naturally enough, that is the way the world appeared to the subject, and he experienced difficulty, as would be expected, in his movements and activity. After some time, however, the field of vision became unsettled, and soon thereafter, everything was straightened around. The subject had adjusted to the distorted stimuli, and "saw" them as undistorted.[4] Apparently, the subject's "expectation" that the world appear as he normally expected it to was able to compensate for perceptual stimuli that reported it as being another way. In a somewhat similar kind of instance, it has also been noted that change in stimuli is essential in order to maintain perception—so essential that if a subject is deprived for a longer period of time of all stimuli, he will himself produce them in the form of visions, auditory hallucinations, and the like.[5] In other words, the intention in this instance not only influences perception, it supplies it. All of this would seem to show, then, that man, far from being passive in the process of perception, is an active, even aggressive subject, and he plays a large, even decisive part, in the perceptual process.

As a matter of fact, were it not for this activity on the part of the receiver of stimuli, he would simply be overwhelmed by the continuous bombardment of an almost infinite variety of perceptual stimuli. In the course of walking around a chair, set in the middle of a room, for example, the variations in light intensity, color shadings, perspectival variations, and the like mean that with every movement of the perceiving subject an almost totally different combination of stimuli is being received. The fact that the chair retains any continuity for the subject in the midst of this bewildering variation of stimuli is the result, not of the chair itself, or of the stimuli, but of the one perceiving the chair. And in fact, it takes quite a bit of perceptual organization to recognize in that kaleidoscopic presentation any firm "object" at all. In other words, such stimulation does not yield a mass of disparate sensations to the perceiver. Those stimuli, rather, appear as organized, and such organization is due to the one receiving the stimuli. Thus, the ordered world of perception, with its stability, regularity, and recognizability, is in large measure due to the organizing power of the percipient.[6]

This is apparent even on the most basic level. Physicists have discovered that the atoms of which our world is composed are mostly space. Yet we perceive objects composed of atoms as solid. It can be determined by measurement that the different colors we see are based on variables within the range of electromagnetic wavelengths to which our eyes will respond. That is, these differences are, physically, simply differences in quantity. Yet we perceive the different colors not in terms of quantity, but in terms of quality. We do not think of red as a little less green. We perceive them as qualitatively different. It is thus rather clear that our world appears to us as it does at least as much because of the way we organize and interpret the stimuli we receive, as because that is the "way things are."

Some of this organization and interpretation is automatic. Our sensory organs, for example, are selective with respect to the kind of stimuli to which they will respond. The ear will "hear" as "sound" only those wavelengths of energy which fall within certain limits. Sounds that are "higher" or "lower" are simply not reported. There is only a limited range of light frequency to which our eyes will respond; we cannot see "infrared" or "ultraviolet" because they fall beyond the limits of that range. Both the "unreported" sounds and sights are there in the form of energy; they are simply "sorted out" by our sensory organs. Perhaps this is to be explained biologically. That is, our organs respond only to those stimuli which aeons of evolution have shown to be necessary for survival. Whether or not that be the case, it is true that some of our perceptions, at least, are affected biologically. For example, a young boy, who moves within a world in which sexual differentiation plays a very minor role, will suddenly be aware of a whole new range of perceptual stimuli after he has gone through puberty. Here, biological changes open to him a whole new area of perception, to which he was previously all but oblivious.

There is also evidence to indicate that experience plays a role in the way perceptions are organized. Experiments with people who were blind from birth because of congenital cataract, and who regained sight after surgical removal of the visual obstruction, indicate that it takes a long period of time before such a person is able to differentiate, for example, between a triangle and a circle with any degree of consistency.[7] In other words, the art of differentiating between various stimuli is, to a certain extent, at least, the result of experience. In fact, it may be that most of the ways in which a person organizes his sensations, his perceptions, is due to his experience with his world. The person discovers that certain ways of organizing perception "work" within the world of objects. That is, from the infinite variety of possible perceptions, a person learns which ones to pay attention to, and how to interpret them, so they help him to function in an acceptable way. Through experience, then, one learns to expect certain patterns of perception in certain circumstances, because they have occurred that way in similar circumstances in the past.

But that would mean that as a result of such experience, a person will not only impose certain patterns on perception, but that, given the start of such a pattern, the person will expect it to be fulfilled, and will tend to reject, or ignore, perceptions that point to the contrary. This has been shown to occur in the so-called "Ames demonstrations," named for the psychologist who created them. These experiments, which combine familiar shapes in such a way as to present the viewer with a perception that seems familiar but is not (e.g., a room whose back wall recedes from the observer from right to left, but whose windows are so constructed as to give the impression that the wall is equidistant at both ends from the observer; a trapezoidal surface, painted to look like a normal, rectangular window seen from an angle, has a rod inserted through it, and is then rotated), demonstrate that the viewer will "see" these objects in ways that are compatible with his assumptions about what they are, and will be confused when they do not act that way. But the confusion remains; the objects are not recognized for what they are, since experience apparently leads the subject to ignore the possibility of "seeing" the objects as distorted representations of familiar things.[8] Habits of perception appear to be so active in this case as to preclude the subject from seeing these things as they "really are," even when perceptions occur that indicate that those objects do not function as one would expect the familiar object to function. Here the intentionality of perception is clearly demonstrated.

In addition to the biological structure of sense organs and the accumulated perceptual experience, there is another factor that influences perception. That is the context within which something is perceived. That is demonstrated by the "optical illusions" with which most people are familiar. Two lines of equal length, for example, can be made to seem unequal by putting arrow "heads" at each end of the top line, and arrow "tails" at each end of the line below. Or two parallel lines can appear to be curved, the top upward and the bottom downward, by superimposing them on a series of lines that cross at the same point, a point located between the two parallel lines (a sort of enlarged asterisk). Similarly, a color can appear to alter its shade simply by putting it beside one color, and then beside another (e.g., a gray circle against a purple background, and then a yellow one). All of this shows rather clearly that the context within which perception occurs will play a large part in determining what that perception will be. In these experiments, a change in context alters the perception.

What all of this shows is simply that man is quite clearly not passive in the act of perception, nor is there a one-to-one relationship between a given object and its perception in all cases. Man's biological structure limits the range of stimuli to which he may respond, while his experience will lead him to expect that the limited stimuli to which he can respond will regularly form themselves in ways he has learned to expect. And he will tend to impose that form on the stimuli even when they do not justify it. The context within which all of this occurs, whether that context is in the form of the stimuli themselves (e.g., the optical illusions) or in the form of expectation of what is to be perceived, will influence the way perception occurs. Perceptual "input" is strongly influenced by what the receiver is prepared, biologically, habitually, and contextually, to receive.

All of this has some rather clear implications concerning the nature of "objective reality," and our relationship to it. If it is true, as we said at the outset of our discussion, that our relationship to the world around us is mediated by our sensory impressions, then the world that surrounds us, the world we perceive, owes at least as much to the intentionality and organizing capacity of perception as it does to the world "out there." Whatever else the various experiments in perception have shown, they do clearly indicate that perception is never "a sure thing, never an absolute revelation of 'what is.' "[9] Rather, everything we perceive is affected not only by what we are physically capable of perceiving but also by our expectation of what forms such perceptions can assume. And this, in turn, limits our ability to experience anything radically different from our previous expectations and habits. In a real sense, "reality" as we know it is dependent on the percipient to give it the structure and the organization that it has. That is not to say, of course, that nothing exists apart from the percipient. Of course it does; our daily experience with the "real" confirms that fact. But the total impression we have of the total collection of "real things," for which I have used the word "reality," does not exist apart from the percipient. Apart from the organization imposed on the welter of sensations with which man is bombarded, there is no "reality," i.e., no organized structure of the "real." Or at least it does not exist in any way we can get at it, apart from the organizing capacity of our own perceptions.[10]

What is more, there is evidence to indicate that people will differ with respect to which set of stimuli they accord priority when confronted with two sets of stimuli that conflict with one another. In an experiment to see whether or not it is possible to determine what constitutes verticality when the only visible frame of reference gives a distorted picture, it was discovered that some people judged the verticle by the visible frame of reference to the exclusion of any kinesthetic sensations that would conflict with the visible stimuli, while others ignored the visible frame of reference, and relied on the kinesthetic. That seems to mean that reality will tend to appear differently to different people, and they will react accordingly, depending on which set of (possibly conflicting) stimuli is accorded priority.[11]

Our "world," therefore, our impression of an organized whole of reality, is in a sense the creation of the way in which we perceive the real, with that perception influenced by habit and expectation. And that is, of course, the only "world," the only "reality" we know, and it is the reality in reference to which we live our lives, make our decisions, and find such meaning as we can in life. It is clear that any change in the way we perceive reality, or the way we "weight" those perceptions, preferring one set to another, will change not only the way we organize our world, but the way we respond to it as well.[12] But we are getting a bit ahead of ourselves with such an observation.

We saw above that the context within which a stimulus occurs will affect the way in which perception occurs. If the context leads a person to expect one stimulus and another is presented, the stimulus presented is not perceived, or at least not so readily. Similarly, if a person expects a certain kind of stimulus, the threshold of perception (i.e., the point at which conscious perception occurs) will be lower than for the identical stimulus occurring in a context in which it is not expected. We also saw how such a context is often provided by the way in which a person organizes his "world" (i.e., the many individual stimuli) into some sort of coherent whole. In other words, the total frame of reference within which a person operates will have profound effects on what and how he perceives. Now one of the major instruments enabling a person to create such a "world" is language. In a sense, language represents the means whereby we are able to profit from the experience of uncounted generations who have similarly faced the task of bringing an ordered world out of the infinite chaos of possible perceptions.

Here again, experiments have shown the way in which language affects one's perception of reality. In one instance, college students were told in one of their classes that a substitute instructor would be present that day, and were given some written information about the new person. Half the class were informed in this way that the instructor was "a rather cold person," the other that he was "warm" and friendly. This context not only influenced the way the students reacted to the new man but also colored their subsequent written evaluation of him.[13] Everyone is of course familiar with similar events demonstrating the suggestibility of human nature, and of course prejudice is a clear manifestation of the way language can provide the context within which perception occurs, thus affecting the perception. Another example is the kind of ambiguous picture, in which two different images are contained, but in which the background tends to obscure one. It will often happen that one of those images will not emerge until it is described; then it seems to leap out from its background, and becomes clearly visible.[14] In this instance, also, language has functioned as the "context" of perception, enabling the person to perceive something not previously noted. There is even some perplexing evidence that man is so sensitive to language that he can respond to the meaning and the emotional connotations of a word that he cannot yet consciously identify.[15] If that does happen, then language obviously could, and would, provide context for perception on a far deeper, and more pervasive, level than conscious verbalization and hearing or reading.

On another level, language seems to represent the sedimented habits of perception that have been developed in interaction with a given environment over a long period of time. That is, language will prepare the person using it for the kind of perception necessary for successful functioning in his own environment. It is reported, for example, that there is a language called Iakuti in which one word is used to describe the colors we call "green" and "blue." Obviously, the distinction between these two colors does not play a significant role in the lives of those who speak this tongue. It would be too much to say that as a result, they perceive no difference between the two, even though their linguistic response to both would be identical. But it may well be that their ability to perceive distinctions, say, within the blue spectrum would not be as highly refined as for a language that can differentiate between navy and royal blue.[16] If that were the case, it would be further indication that a person's linguistic framework would have an effect on his perception by preparing him to expect certain differentiations that another language would not lead him to expect. And the result of such expectations, as we saw, would in all likelihood affect what is, and is not, perceived. That is, language may well function as the total context within which perception occurs, in which case it would, as context, have rather telling effect on what will and will not be perceived.

It would appear, therefore, that language plays a key role in man's relationship to reality, in the way he perceives it, understands it, and reacts to it. If, as we have said, it is in fact the percipient who organizes and selects the stimuli to which he responds, and responds to them in ways determined both biologically and habitually, then language will play a key part in organizing the perceived stimuli into a totality. Perception is, after all, an experience of limited duration, and is not itself capable of creating an organized totality from the stimuli that are perceived. It is therefore in all likelihood language that transforms experience into a "universe of discourse," into a frame of reference within which all perceptions take on meaning.

In fact, this very assignment of "meaning" to the world thus created is another of the key functions of language. The ability to compare perceptions with one another, and to arrive at judgments regarding them depends on the possibility of abstracting from the immediate moment a given perception, and comparing it with others received at other times. But this is precisely the function of language. It enables man to describe, and thus to fix, a given perception, so that it may be recalled at a later time, and compared with other perceptions similarly fixed. It is this totality of fixed perceptions that constitutes man's world, that provides the context within which perception occurs, and which thus leads him to expect certain kinds of perception, and not others.

A language appears, therefore, to be the sedimentation into words of the collective experience of a given people. It provides a perspective on the world, and thus colors the way in which that world will be perceived. It is for that reason that translation from one language into another is never completely successful. Something is quite literally "lost in the translation," namely, a way of looking at the world.

Language is also the way in which man becomes master of the universe. Only when the kind of abstraction from the daily flow of events that becomes possible through language occurs, can we arrive at ways of manipulating, even creating, new forms of reality. Language allows us to abstract items from the flow of perceptions and compare them with one another, as we noted above. Thus, language makes possible the derivation and expression of such a formula as $E = MC^2$, and in the wake of that language there follows the atomic age. It would be fair to say, in fact, that, in the sense that language enables man to deal with reality in such a way, language not only organizes, it creates reality for man. But that is true in a broader sense, as well. The very concept of "reality," implying a coherent structure, is the result of the organizing capacity inherent in language. Therefore, apart from language, the possibility of discovering, and then imposing upon the "real," a unity or coherence would be strictly limited, if not impossible. In that way, language creates "reality."[17] A primitive mind, for example, that does not function in terms of the law of contradiction, so evident to us because of the structure of our language, will then experience reality in an entirely different way from Western man who is dominated by that law of contradiction. If language does not lead one to expect reality to function in certain specific ways, one's experience of reality will be quite different from that experienced by one who does expect it.[18] Language, functioning as context, will play a large part in determining what is, indeed what can be, perceived. In that sense, therefore, reality is a function of language.

It would also seem a fair inference from all of this to conclude that man is indeed a linguistic being. At the heart of what differentiates him from all other animate forms on the earth, whether it is the ability to perform abstractions, make tools, or respond to humor, lies language, which permits him to deal with reality in a way open to no non-linguistic creature. Indeed, one could perhaps even say that the world is what it is for man because man is capable of language.[19]

In the light of our discussion of the relationship between perception, language, and reality, it can be understood why any theological movement that takes such a relationship into account ought to be given serious attention. Let us again point out that we do not think we have established, on an empirical basis, the truth or validity of any such theological approach. What we have tried to do is simply to show that great emphasis on language as the constitutive element of human nature does not represent a gross distortion in understanding the way a man becomes human or functions as a human being in the world.

PART TWO

THE NEW HERMENEUTIC

WE HAVE NOW INVESTIGATED the nature of our problem; we have reviewed a way of carrying on philosophy, and the way one theologian used some of those philosophical concepts in interpreting the Christian faith; and we have looked at the role that language plays in man's relationship to the world. We are now ready to examine in some detail the new hermeneutic in an effort to determine whether or not it is a viable solution to the hermeneutical problem. We shall undertake our investigation by looking first at some basic suppositions about the nature of man and language, and the nature of faith, which are held by the new hermeneutic. We shall then be in a position to consider the way in which the text is to be approached, in the light of those suppositions, and to examine the kind of exegetical and hermeneutical results that may be obtained in that way. Finally, we shall attempt to see the new hermeneutic in its relationship to its background, and evaluate some of the results that this way of looking at the New Testament has achieved.

6

Man and Language

ALTHOUGH A NUMBER of scholars, in Germany as well as in the
United States, have taken an active part in the movement that
has come to be called the "new hermeneutic," the two persons
with whom this theological approach is most closely associated
are Ernst Fuchs and Gerhard Ebeling. Professor Fuchs was born
in the southern part of Germany in 1903 and carried on his
theological studies at the time when the dialectical theology was
in its earliest stages. Among others, Professor Fuchs studied
with Adolf Schlatter, and with Martin Heidegger and Rudolf
Bultmann when both taught at Marburg. After some years in
the pastorate, Professor Fuchs taught in the universities of Tübingen and Berlin and then became professor of New Testament
in Marburg. Professor Ebeling, a few years younger than Fuchs
(he was born in 1912) also studied with Bultmann in Marburg,
and was also a pastor before he began his teaching career. Although Professor Ebeling began in the field of church history,
he undertook in 1954 to teach in the field of systematic theology. His career has been divided between the universities of
Tübingen, in southern Germany, and Zurich, in Switzerland.
Perhaps it is because both had served as pastors during a very
difficult time in the life of the German Church (during the
National Socialist period) that they share an emphasis on the
need for effective proclamation of the gospel. Many of the
themes that engage the attention of the new hermeneutic will

be more easily understood if this is kept sight of as the goal toward which the movement points. We must now examine some of those themes and the problems that they seek to answer.

One way of approaching the fundamental problem with which the new hermeneutic is concerned is to see it in terms of the question about the communicability of revelation.[1] Granted the assertion that events did occur in which, or through which, God revealed himself and his purposes, how are we to understand that revelation so that it is not limited in significance to the immediate period in which it occurred? What will the nature of that revelation have to have been, if it is to be communicable after the death of those who experienced it firsthand, and the demise of the historical age in which it occurred? The New Testament, of course, does not imply that revelation of God, or activity by God for man, ended with the career of Jesus of Nazareth. The affirmation of his resurrection is in itself enough to lay any such idea to rest. However such continuing activity may be conceived, the New Testament, and with it the Christian theologian, still sees something of normative value in the events surrounding Jesus. Yet unless something of the content of those events is known, they cannot function in any normative capacity. Therefore, something of the revelation, at least, must be communicable beyond the period in which Jesus lived, if he is in any way to be normative for the Christian faith. The problem of what that revelation is, and how it can be communicated, is the problem with which the new hermeneutic concerns itself, and it is, rather obviously, a problem basic to any understanding of the Christian faith. Whatever the new hermeneutic can contribute to the solution of that problem will have implications for theology as a whole.

For that reason, the new hermeneutic has not limited itself merely to questions concerning the technique of interpreting an ancient document (the New Testament). Rather, there are implications for systematic theology, as well as church history and practical theology, in the way the new hermeneutic approaches, and seeks to solve, this basic question. The proponents of the new hermeneutic, in some instances, are quite prepared to in-

vade the precincts of philosophy, so broad is their understanding
of the implications of their approach. The new hermeneutic is
therefore not limited to exegesis; it is a way of doing theology,
and it will be better understood if that is kept in mind. Otherwise, much of what is said will seem to wander far from the
more limited task of interpreting New Testament texts, and
will seem to lack exegetical justification. Further, because it is
a way of doing theology, the new hermeneutic will at times
seem to move in ways for which insufficient exegetical warrant
is provided, had its proponents intended to limit themselves
merely to such interpreting. Rather, the new hermeneutic, as a
way of approaching theology, is, its proponents would argue,
based on sound exegesis but not limited merely to an exposition of texts. "Interpretation" (hermeneutic) means making
sense of (and thus interpreting) human existence rather than
simply deciphering texts, and to carry out such a program the
new hermeneutic sets its sights on the whole area of theology.

If, then, the task is to make sense of human existence, it is
obvious that a prime requisite will be some understanding of
what man is and how he functions. Since this is precisely the
kind of question with which the philosophy of Martin Heidegger deals, and since Bultmann has already demonstrated the
potential contained in that way of carrying on philosophy for
dealing with certain theological questions, it ought not to be
too surprising to find that Heidegger's influence is also at work
here.[2] An investigation of the way the new hermeneutic understands, and describes, man's nature may therefore yield rather
familiar results.

When one speaks of the "nature" of man (a phrase that in
itself has connotations entirely alien to this kind of approach
for which man has no substantive "nature"), one inevitably
deals with the problem of how man becomes truly a self. The
task of the self is simply to become a true self, and its goal is
reached, however provisionally, when such selfhood is attained.
All of this is clear enough, for example, in Heidegger's thought.
This has as its result the fact that the key question, so far as
man is concerned, is the question of self-understanding. That

is, What does man take himself to be? The answer to that will determine where he attempts to go, which in turn will determine whether or not selfhood is achieved. Furthermore, in order really to achieve valid self-understanding, one must know the alternatives for understanding himself which are available to him.[3] Only in that way can valid self-understanding, and thus true selfhood, be achieved. Lest there be any misunderstanding on the meaning of self-understanding, however, Fuchs contrasts it with self-consciousness. Self-consciousness refers to the ability of man to react as man in any given situation, and can serve as a sort of catalyst in bringing out what a man can or cannot do as the man he is. Self-understanding, on the other hand, refers to the position a man has assumed over against his historic situation, i.e., how much of what is "self-understood" or obvious in a given culture also operates axiomatically in his own life. Thus, self-understanding, in terms of such a stand, needs continually to be reaffirmed, and represents, in a sense, the task the self poses for itself. Man's self-consciousness as man could hardly be changed without transforming him into something other than a human being; his self-understanding will be changed when he takes up a different position vis-à-vis his historic situation.[4]

All of that means, of course, that the self is not a static entity. Nothing about the self is ever really, finally, totally completed. There is always something lying ahead, something still to come, so long as man is alive. Put another way, it means that man, to be man, always has a future. And so long as that is the case, he always has his selfhood before him as a task. That also means that man is oriented to the future in such a way that he draws his very being as man from the future. Even his past is never secure. Something can happen in the future that will turn something deemed triumph into defeat, or vice versa. Thus, the future is determinative even for the past. Whatever selfhood the man may have achieved in the past is constantly called into question by the future into which he advances.[5]

This open-endedness of man to the future has at least three consequences. First of all, it means that in a real sense the future, or more broadly, time, is the basis of human existence.

Man must learn "what it is time for," if he is to act appropriately in the face of the future coming upon him.[6] Secondly, it means that man is always open to question. He can never rest on his past achievements; history continually calls his historic achievement of selfhood into question. The future thus stands as both threat and promise to man; it gives him renewed opportunity to achieve selfhood, and threatens to nullify what he has achieved in the past. The point at which this reality of the future as a confused voice of both promise and threat comes to focus is man's conscience. It is there that the future already begins to stir in him.[7] Thirdly, it means that man is called upon to respond to this future which continually comes to him. Man lives, as it were, between this call and his response to it. This response must come in the form of a decision as to how to react to, and make use of, the opportunities that the future presents to man.[8]

If all that is true, the one point it all centers down on is man's decision that he must make vis-à-vis the future. It is there that existence takes place. If time is the basis of human existence, then the reality of that existence is precisely that decision. And it is decision, ultimately, on the meaning and significance of the world for the self. Confronted with the future as it opens itself to him, man must decide what meaning, in the light of these events bearing down upon him, the world will have for him. Put another way, it means that he must decide how he will understand himself in relation to the world the future brings to him.[9] That does not mean that everything that occurs in the course of day-to-day living is equally decisive. But "historic events" do demand such decisions, and historic events are those events which demand that some stand be taken with regard to them. Such a stand then exerts influence on the way life is carried on, i.e., on the person's self-understanding. Man, therefore, open to a future that demands he respond to it in the form of decision, namely, the decision as to its meaning for him, must therefore recognize those events which are vital to him, and must decide appropriately.

There are some implications to this way of looking at man

that need to be considered. It presumes, for example, that man is able to understand the meaning of himself, his world, and the historic events that the future brings, if he is to carry out his task of achieving selfhood. If understanding were not a basic characteristic of human existence, man would simply not be, nor could he become, man. Understanding, therefore, is a fundamental mode of activity in achieving existence.[10] But such understanding in its turn presumes the availability of some sort of language by means of which such understanding may be accomplished.

A second implication of this whole position consists in the observation that man, who receives the basis of his existence (the future, time) from outside himself, is therefore not his own creator. He is summoned to be himself by something outside himself. It means that every man lives in dependency. Man's experience of existence leads him to be aware that there is a power that has man in its grip, and over which man can exercise no final control. That power is God. Every man is thus dependent upon God, and cannot achieve true selfhood except in the light of that fact.[11]

If that is the case, then it is clear that ignorance of the dependence on God would keep a person from achieving authentic self-understanding. He would always react to the future in terms of a self that cannot exist, i.e., a self independent of God. Thus, a "sinner" is incapable of achieving any kind of valid self-understanding.[12] But how is that fact to be communicated to him? Obviously, again, the question of language is posed, this time including the question of the relationship between language and God. It is therefore clearly necessary that we turn our attention to investigating the nature and function of language.

Language, as far as the new hermeneutic is concerned, does not represent an arbitrary choice of vocal sounds to represent certain things that man runs up against "out there." Rather, event and word are born together, and are not to be understood in any other way. That means that an event needs the words, the language, it calls forth in order to be itself. We could call

this event-word unity a "word-event" or "language-event." The
language thus given birth illumines the reality that summoned
it forth, so that, in terms of man's existence, the purpose of the
word, of language, is to lighten the darkness of existence. Thus,
language is itself a hermeneutical entity, illumining the situation into which it is spoken. That means that language, rising
with the event, is a way of meeting reality. Language is the way
man comes to terms with events that the future brings to him.[13]
Thus, as events summon forth words to illumine them, and
these words pass into the language, enriching the possibilities of
illumination contained in language, there is a "language-gain."
That is, language is enriched as more and more responses to
events accrue to a given language.

All of that, in its turn, means that there are embedded in language a variety of responses to events. Put another way, we
could say that language contains the possibilities of self-understanding, and therefore of human existence, as they have found
expression in the past. A language represents the way in which
a people have learned to come to terms with themselves and
with their world, ordering the language, and thus their world, in
the light of their past experience. If, as we have seen, man, to
be man, must achieve his existence by decision in the light of
the future, and in the light of the possibilities of human existence open to him, then it follows that he must turn to language (history!) to learn of those possibilities. Thus, in a real
sense, man as man lives from language, as it offers to him possibilities of meeting and illumining events as they come to him.[14]

To illustrate this point, Fuchs speaks of a garden that has,
through neglect, grown over. A man, coming upon such a garden,
may either attempt to restore it or he may leave it as it is. In
either case, however, the garden shows him what once did exist
as a way of gardening. In the same way, language, as response
to events of central meaning for a way of looking at life (therefore, "language-events"), shows us the contours of what human
existence has been understood to be. It shows man what once
existed as a way of understanding, and carrying on, human ex-

istence. It also shows us a way we could carry on our existence, if we so chose. Because man draws such possible ways of existing from his language, he is in a real sense created by that language. Man is not the creator, he is the creature, of language, and he lives on the possibilities it discloses to him.[15]

This has an important consequence. It means that man is limited, in the range of possible ways of existing, to those possibilities contained in his language. In that way, language operates as a man's fate, limiting him, in his particular period in history, to the responses that have been made to the events that preceded him. That different periods of history will offer him, through language as it exists in that period, differing possibilities, is clear enough. Thus, language is man's fate, determining the limits of the possibilities within which man has to work, and thus in a sense limiting what the man can become as man. By being limited in its own historic period, language in turn limits man to the possibilities that language at that historical moment can offer. Both understanding and human existence are thus functions of history, and that means of language.[16]

Not only is human existence a function of language, however. All "reality" is determined by language. If we define reality as "what is," we must note in the verb "is" the present tense, argues Fuchs. That is, it belongs to reality that it "be" "now," that it be capable of presence, if only a remembered (or anticipated) presence. Further, if that reality is to be grasped, its presence, and my presence, must coincide. The only way that can happen is in language, which is capable, through the tenses of its verbs, of conferring presence, either current, remembered, or anticipated. If something cannot be named or spoken, it is to that extent unreal for man. Thus, Fuchs concludes, reality is a function of language. Putting it another way, one could say that for reality to function as reality for man, it must be *understood* as reality, yet it is equally obvious to say that understanding happens only by means of language. As a result, apart from language, there is no reality, at least none that would function as such for man.[17]

If it is true, as we saw earlier, that time is the basis of human existence, an existence that is nothing if not linguistic; and if it is true that reality itself depends on language to confer "presence" on it, so it may function as reality for man, and not pass unnoticed in the undifferentiated stream of things, then, by inference, language and time are intimately related. That is true to the extent that Fuchs, for example, can argue that the purpose of language is to announce "what it is time for." In the use of language in the family, for example, where language has not been debased to the point of simply providing "objective" information, in which no one is existentially involved, language contains this characteristic: "it is time to eat," "time to practice," "time for bed," and the like.[18]

A further inference to be drawn from this discussion on the nature of language consists in the observation that language, functioning properly, lets things be, or denies them such being. A word motivated by hate excludes the existence of the one so addressed from the "world" of the speaker, as a word of love grants such being. That is, language defines, and thus allows, the world to function as world. But here we have come upon what for Fuchs is a key point about language, namely, that whatever the words, whether they permit or deny, whether they be words of love or of hate, they are based, and must be if they are to be effective, on a prior "agreement" or "consent" among men. The word that we have translated "agreement" or "consent" is in German *Einverständnis*. It has the connotation of both English words, but, equally importantly, contains in itself the word for "understanding," i.e., *Verständnis*. It is for that reason a most useful word for a theology that places as much emphasis on the role of understanding (e.g., self-understanding, understanding what it is time for, etc.) as does the new hermeneutic.[19]

If, therefore, it is true that language can create understanding, it is profoundly true that only where such understanding already exists can language function at all. Otherwise there would be no coincidence of language and words between men; apart from any common basis, all language would be talking to oneself. That does not, of course, mean that all men agree on all things, or that they even agree in what they say. Yet communication, by language or any other means, would be totally impossible apart from some common basis. If a word of hate or exclusion is to be effective, there must be agreement that it *is* a word of hate. Even more, if language is as crucial for human existence as has been argued, then agreement (on which effective language is based) is what makes man, man. Therefore, the event of agreement underlies both human existence and language. They both have this common root.

A further consequence of this "agreement" which underlies language consists in the fact that when language functions properly, it allows "Being" to others, it creates "room" within which other things can function as well. That is, in "agreement," an individual withdraws himself, as it were, from an area which he thus opens to another, an area within which the other may function. This clearing of a space for another happens in language, since the very existence of language, based on agreement, implies permission for another to function. Thus, Being is a linguistic event, but even more, since language is based on agreement that allows others to be, i.e., language denies the self the room within which another may function and is thus self-giving, that original agreement may be defined as "Being realized through language as love."

That has a number of consequences. For instance, language creates community, by permitting men to exist side by side, by means of the room that language creates for others. Language grants the self to others by giving permission to the other to call upon the self when the other is in need. The characteristic of language is therefore to impart, whether it is the impartation of Being or reality, or of room for another to function in one's world, or the self imparting itself to another when the other has need. It can be summed up by saying that language is the arena within which love, peace, and joy function.[20] If this is in fact the true nature of language, then it will not be too difficult to understand the claim Fuchs will make a bit later that the Christian faith simply follows the "inner tendency" of language. Language and faith clearly seem to be "made for each other"!

On the basis of such an understanding of the nature and function of language, furthermore, it is not hard to see why it should be insisted that the nature of "word," or language, is not so much speech as act. Language, it has been argued, is grounded in the same place as man—in agreement—and therefore language has the power to make man and community, to create space for love and peace, or it also has the power to destroy. Therefore words are events in their ability to "touch and change our very life," and we get at their nature only by asking what they effect, what they set in motion. For that reason, communication between two persons is a matter not only of the content of language but of the effect such communication has on people. Words of joy communicated to another do not convey simply a content, they convey the very joy of the one who is communicating. Hence, argues Ebeling, "word" in its essence is encounter, and as encounter, it involves at least two persons. Thus the basic structure of word is not to be a statement *about* something; when a word becomes that, it has already become abstracted from its reality, and has fallen into a kind of neutral jargon incapable of real communication. Rather, "word" is an event in which people participate in their common reality with one another, an event in which man in fact becomes man along with his fellows.[21]

All of this also makes it clear why, for the new hermeneutic, language itself is capable of being the key to theology. If word, and language, are in fact capable of, and characterized by, the kind of power that has just been claimed for them, then it is not hard to see how the relationship between God and man, and man and man, takes place in and through language. If word is essentially act, then it is clear that for God to speak would mean that he acts, and the inference that "His speaking is the way of his acting" lies close at hand.[22] But even more, if language is capable, as we have seen, of creating room for others, and of granting them this room, through language, by granting permission to another to call upon the self when the other has need, then language is quite capable of functioning as the Word of God which communicates God to man. Language functions as an encounter between God and man, creating for man room in which to live, and giving man permission to call on God when man has need. That is as much as to say that to speak of the Word of God is not to speak of some special kind of language, apart from human language, which is somehow spoken into human language, and then, as the case may be, corrupted or preserved, lost or proclaimed. Rather, the Word of God means language, word, functioning as it ought to function. Thus, "Word of God" does not mean a special or supernatural word, but "true, proper, finally valid word."[23]

This also means that the word is the only possible means of revelation, if God is to come into man's situation in such a way that human response to and participation in that coming not only are to be possible but can be expected without further question. Only if God can impart himself to man, thus creating love and community, in such a way that man can participate in it without being destroyed as man, or his response becoming something other than a human response, can God really come to *man*. It is apparent that the place in which all of this can occur is in language.[24] This also then solves the problem of the communicability of revelation; if revelation occurs in language, without altering or destroying the structure of human language, then wherever language is possible, revelation can be communicated. Since language forms the point of contact, as it were, between God and man, and since revelation of God to man thus occurs in language, as event, indeed as "word-event," then that revelation can continue to operate, as "word-event," wherever language, true language, remains a possibility.

Given all this, there are implications for the way theology is to be carried out which are contained in this view of the nature and function of language, which we must examine if we are to see why the new hermeneutic functions the way it does.

The first implication has to do with the definition and task of hermeneutics. We have seen that language itself is already an interpretation of existence. That is, language does not point to some reality that exists apart from any experience of it and that is available even apart from language. Language does not make statements *about* such an "objective" reality; rather, language conveys the way in which a person views, and understands, or interprets life. Such an interpretation is available in no other way than through the language in which it is expressed. In this sense, language alone is capable of making available to me the reality of another's way of understanding life, its meaning and its goal.

But language does not arise only when one person wants to communicate the meaning of his life, or of some event in that life, to another. Rather, language is the response to an event by means of which the man who confronts it seeks to understand the event, and to fit it into his world, so that it may continue to function as event, and as reality, for him. Language is thus born in the attempt to understand, to "interpret" (to oneself or to others), the meaning of human life, of existence. That means that any really adequate "interpretation" or understanding of the language contained in a text will not be so much an attempt to clarify the meaning of the language itself, as though by such clarification we could then get at whatever it is that the text describes, but which exists apart from, and is available apart from, the text. Rather, such a true interpretation will be an attempt to see what interpretation of reality, of existence, that language is trying to make clear. The language of a text has not been interpreted, therefore, until its meaning for man's existence has been discerned. Interpretation is thus not so much my clarification of an obscure text, so that it makes sense, as it is the text's clarification of human existence. The "object" of clarification, of interpretation, is therefore human existence, not some object to which the language of the text points, or about which it seeks to convey some piece of information.

Further, since the text contains an interpretation of existence, the text will demand a decision from me as to whether or not I accept its interpretation of existence as valid for me. Therefore, the central task of any interpretation will be to carry on the interrogations of the text's interpretation of existence in such a way that both the interrogation and its results remain related to existence. Any understanding of the text that points to some reality with which I may or may not become involved, or in which I may, if I please, remain disinterested, since it is, after all, a reality that does not really concern me, will be a false understanding. If a true understanding of the text *must* be related to human existence, then that means that a basic task of the new hermeneutic will be to provide the concepts that such an interpretation needs so that its results will not be divorced from existence. That is, when we question the text which, as language, is itself the clarification of the meaning of an event for existence, we must take care that the meaning of the text be stated in such a way that the meaning for existence of the event of which the text is an expression, and the decision it demands of me about my existence, are not lost sight of.[25]

Moreover, if man lives from the historical possibilities of existence that language offers him, and if he is to find out from a text what kind of possibility of existence the text offers him, then the task of hermeneutic will be to find the way the text needs to be questioned to yield such results. That is, hermeneutics must provide a framework within which the text can be understood as a linguistic response to existence, and thus as a possible response on my part to existence as well. If the text is to help me in my effort to illuminate reality through my own language, then it must be asked the kind of questions that will cause the text to answer in ways that illumine existence. Thus, one will not want to ask the text, for example, about the "furniture of heaven" or the structure of the word, or the overall plan of history. One will ask the text about human existence, since that is what one needs to know. Therefore, the new hermeneutic must provide the existential questions that will allow the text to function as what it is, i.e., as a linguistic response to, and illumination of, existence.[26]

If all that is true, then a second consequence follows, namely, that anything in the text that hinders the text from functioning as an illumination of existence, or seems to do so, must be interpreted not the way it seems to require to be, but must be so questioned that it does answer in existential terms. Myth is precisely such an element in the New Testament. Myth does in fact seem to present a picture of objective reality, in terms of the way the universe is structured (a three-storied universe, a seven-layered heaven, etc.). That is, myth seems to be trying to give information about the way the universe is constructed, something that hardly demands any kind of existential participation or decision as response. For that reason, the new hermeneutic must continue the task of demythologizing. It must be done because myth is, as the new hermeneutic understands it, the enemy of the gospel. It is that for a variety of reasons. Let us isolate but two.

On the one hand, human existence is, as we saw, grounded in time. It is constituted by the future in the face of which it must make its decisions, and it draws its possibilities from the linguistic deposit of the past, a linguistic deposit that itself, as language, is primarily concerned with time, since, as we saw, language gives "presence"[27] to reality, and has as its purpose the telling of time—what it is time for. Myth, on the other hand, knows nothing of time. It seeks to picture the timeless truth of eternal validity, which in itself hardly represents a response to existence, or the demand for a decision in the light of a possible illumination of existence. Thus, myth knows nothing of time,[28] and must therefore be either interpreted in terms useful to illumining human existence or ignored completely. On the other hand, myth seeks to force reality into its own "concepts." It is not open to event, but seeks to set the stage within which an event can happen. Thus, just as man can use concepts to force truth into pre-determined channels, thus "objectifying," and falsifying, a reality that is fundamentally existential and demands decision and participation, so myth tends to objectify and falsify such existential truth.[29] Language is communication, participation; and demythologizing means simply to restore to language that, its primal function: hearing and delivering communication that reflects life, rather than merely bearing information.[30]

In the light of all this (the third consequence), the interpretation of the text is not complete until the text again becomes a linguistic illumination of existence. That is to say, interpretation is not complete until the text is proclaimed. In the sermon, in proclamation, the text becomes an aid in interpreting existence as it confronts us.[31] Preaching is uniquely suited to be the final outcome of interpreting the New Testament text, since preaching represents, at its best, an announcement about a possible way of interpreting existence, and therefore the demand that the hearer make a decision about it. Proclamation is thus a question that demands decision.[32] It is a linguistic summons to take seriously a word-event, i.e., a linguistic illumination of existence, and to confront the decision as to whether or not that is a possible reaction for me to make.

Therefore, in true proclamation, it is not I who interpret the text by putting its language into modern dress; rather, the text interprets my existence, and asks me to judge my own way of reacting to life in the light of the response that called the text into being. For the new hermeneutic, the text is not something to be measured by our standards of truth or by our mode of existence. Rather, we are called upon to measure our life in the light of the text, and decide whether or not the text is to be accepted as the way we also must respond to existence.

Put in more theological terms, the sermon requires of its hearers the decision of faith, something to which the sermon itself, as linguistic event, gives birth. The new hermeneutic, therefore, seeks to eventuate in the proclamation of faith. In that proclamation, the text, born of the event of faith that summoned forth appropriate language by which that faith could be expressed and understood, may again become language-event for the hearer. When the proclamation of faith does become language-event for the hearer, it teaches him the language of faith, so that he may understand his life in this new way. The proclamation is the question addressed to man, which makes it possible for him to decide for faith. With this preliminary conclusion, we have come upon a further element that plays a key role in the new hermeneutic, namely, faith, and we must now turn to consider it in some detail.

7

Faith

WE SAW in the last chapter how the basic problem of the new hermeneutic, the communicability of revelation, led to some fundamental insights into the way in which man and language are viewed. We saw how these two elements in turn led us to the point where we must consider faith. Perhaps it is needless to point out that our isolation of these various elements is somewhat artificial, since all of these parts fit together into a single whole. Our need in this chapter to discuss again, for example, the nature and function of language is enough to make that clear. Yet of all these elements, faith plays a key role, as will be evident in the fact that what we have discussed thus far has led to it, and in the fact that our discussion of faith in turn will lead us directly into the basic methodological problem of the new hermeneutic, namely, the approach to the text. We are dealing in this chapter, therefore, with a most important theme, an understanding of which will perhaps clarify what at times may seem to be the rather strange positions adopted by the men who attempt to carry out theology within the framework of the new hermeneutic.

We have seen that the fundamental task of the self is to achieve selfhood. It is not surprising, therefore, that faith should be defined in these terms. What may be surprising, however, is the fact that faith is defined as the abandonment of the self. That is, faith is the abandonment of the attempt to determine on one's own what the self is to be, and to seek to justify, to "ground," the self in terms of the world in which it finds itself. Faith is a cessation of self-assertion. It is willingness to let others be as they are, to allow others room in which to exist also.[1] It is, in a sense, an abandonment of the attempt to assert the priority of one's own self at the inevitable expense of others. The result will be a freedom from the necessity of creating one's self, as it were; a freedom from the care and anxiety that invariably attend upon the attempt of the self to act as its own creator.[2]

Since faith has to do with the self in its attempt to exist as a self in the world, it is further evident that faith has to do with the totality of man's existence, not with parts of man, or discrete portions of his life. Faith is not one act or attitude out of many; it is the very substance of the way the whole of life is lived.[3] It would also be wrong, therefore, to try to limit faith to "spiritual matters," or to the "inner" life of an individual. Rather, faith has to do with the way in which man confronts the whole of reality, the way he lives vis-à-vis God and the world.[4]

The task of faith is therefore the continuing interpretation of Christian existence, in the light of the events that confront man in the world.[5] It is quite clear as a result that faith cannot remove one from the vicissitudes of historical existence. Rather, it has the effect of immersing him in history.[6] It is also clear that faith cannot be expounded or systematized once for all. It is not possible to have a "finished model" for faith. Since faith is a way of dealing with life in the world, faith is as open to changing forms and tasks as life itself.[7] But there is a profounder reason for the openness of faith, namely, the fact that faith means precisely the abandonment of trying to secure one's own self and its interests against the kind of changes that history makes necessary and inevitable. Since faith accepts the self and its life as a gift of God (God, not man, is the creator), it is in no position to say what can or cannot ultimately belong to the life of faith. Faith is therefore not the articulation of eternal and unchanging truth(s).[8] It is a willingness to abandon the self to God, and thus to remain open to what he may send in the future.

This does not mean, however, that faith is simply an interpretation of life that life itself seems to require, or that one need only pay attention to the world and its history in order to achieve faith. Quite the contrary. Faith, in fact, can be characterized as believing despite what one sees and experiences in life. In fact, Fuchs argues, faith based on such facts of history would be a rather unstable reality.[9] To be sure, faith needs absolute certainty to be itself, but that certainty is not based simply on observation of the way life in the world proceeds. In fact, any certainty grounded in historical fact would destroy faith, as we shall see in a moment. Rather, faith is continually involved in a struggle to believe. It must continually reaffirm itself in the act of believing. Faith is thus absolute certainty in the face of what is absolutely uncertain, i.e., the future.[10]

If all of that is true, then it is clear that faith is not something that exists far beyond the world of time and change, or that protects the self from ultimate exposure to such temporal instability. Rather, it is precisely such temporal instability, such life, that is the sphere of faith. But there is a more intimate connection between time and faith for the new hermeneutic than simply the statement that time is the sphere within which faith operates. Time is itself the content of faith. That is, when Jesus announced that the Kingdom of God was at hand, he was announcing a new *time* for men, the time to live in the love of God. Faith, therefore, accepts that announcement, and with it, faith accepts this new time, this time of love, as the gift of God. For faith, therefore, time is not simply an unending series of events. Rather, faith accepts time as the gift of God, and thus allows this new time of God's love to determine the way life is to be lived. Put another way, one could say that the gospel is an announcement of time, indeed that that announcement, by its very occurrence, makes time available now as God's gift.[11] To accept that announcement, in faith, means to give up the attempt to have time at one's own disposal, to shape one's life for one's own benefit and on one's own terms. It means to accept time, and what it brings, as coming from God.[12] The basic question of faith, therefore, concerns the way one comports himself with time.

Such comportment with time, however, if in faith such time is accepted as God's gift, means comportment with, and attitude toward, the future. In fact, faith can be defined as a relation to the future, a relation which by its very nature changes the future. This is a key point. Faith does not in some metaphysical way protect the believer from an adverse future, nor does it in some magical way guarantee a secure future. Faith does not even protect one from the most final future of all, death. Rather, faith sees the future as coming from God's hand, and therefore the future becomes quite different, even though it is the same future as that faced by everyone else. Faith allows one to confront, and accept, that future in a way quite different from the way others must confront it. For faith, the future is not threat but promise; it does not threaten destruction, it promises God. The meaning of the future is shown by Christ the Crucified One, which means that the future brings us the victory of God over death, namely, the victory of love. In fact, for this reason, it is only through faith that a genuine future is possible at all. Only in faith can the future be expected to bring anything different than it has brought in the past. Only in faith can the future be seen as God coming to us. For this reason, Ebeling can say that "faith does not 'have' a future, it *is* the future."[13]

It is because faith awaits, and accepts, the future as God's future that the present is also transformed for faith. Because faith accepts the "future of the future" as God rather than death,[14] faith sees the present in a new light, namely, as the arrival of love in the present. And this is precisely the meaning of Jesus. He announced the arrival of the time of God's love, an arrival that faith accepts, and can then see. That means that for faith, the present is not simply a fleeting "now" ever disappearing into the past or not yet arrived from the future. Rather, for faith, the present is the time of love, when all things are brought together in a new way, when in love, all things appear in a new light.[15] In fact, faith may also be defined as love at work. This is what is meant when the New Testament claims that there is no faith without works. Faith is thus effective as love.[16]

Yet at the same time, the presence of love in the present, because love has been determined as the future by God, is not something that can be statistically verified, as it were. Love is not only the substance of faith at work, love also requires faith in order for love to be visible. It is precisely *not* apparent that the present is a time of love. There is *no* evidence from the way man has lived in the past that gives credence to the affirmation that the future of the future is love, rather than self-assertion. For that very reason, love is as dependent on faith as faith is on love. If the victory of love is not apparent in the present, and if there is no reason, on the basis of past and present, to think that love will be the determinant of the future, then we must also say that faith is faith in the victory of love. Only in faith can we assert that the future is God's future, which means a future in which love triumphs over death, and therefore only in faith can we see the present as the time of the arrival, and therefore the presence, of God's love. But where then does faith come from? Where does faith look in order to see, and thus rejoice in, this love? Where is the victory of love evident, which allows faith to expect the future as love, and thus see the present in its light? The answer: in Jesus. Faith believes, as Jesus did, in the victory of love.[17]

It is for this reason that Jesus is central for the Christian faith. Faith believes the truth of the historical interpretation of love that occurred in Jesus. Faith believes in the love that was "objectified" in him.[18] Faith therefore knows itself to be dependent on Jesus Christ. If Jesus had not in fact lived, or if it could be shown that faith in him were based on a gross misunderstanding of the meaning and significance of Jesus, then the Christian faith would clearly have lost its basis and ground.[19] Faith is therefore not the creation of man, nor the reflection of a desire to have things other than they happen to be. Faith clearly depends on Jesus of Nazareth. And it depends on him because in him we see how we must accept life as God's gift, how we must give up the attempt to provide the basis of our own life, how we must abandon our own self-assertion and live in the present as in a time of love. Faith depends on Jesus, therefore, as the one who gives us the measure of the way we are to determine our concrete, everyday life. Whether or not one has faith, therefore, depends on whether or not one can come into "agreement" with Jesus of Nazareth, whether or not he becomes the measure for our life. Faith thus confesses that Jesus occurred "for us" by following his way.[20]

All of this clearly means that Jesus of Nazareth, as he lived and taught, is basic for the Christian faith. Yet there lurks in this relationship to the historical Jesus a grave danger to faith, if this relationship is misunderstood, a danger to which the theologians of the new hermeneutic are most sensitive. In fact, one gets the impression that the question of the relationship between the Jesus of history and faith is one of the most fundamental questions with which the interpreter of the New Testament has to deal. If this relationship between faith and history is misunderstood, faith is perverted to the extent that it can no longer function as faith. We must investigate this problem in some detail, and from several perspectives.

One aspect of the problem concerns the nature of God's word. One of the basic insights of the new hermeneutic concerning the word of God consists in the affirmation that God's word does not provide information of one type or another that man may or may not be interested in, or find useful. Rather, God's word cannot be his word in any objective, detached sense. God's word demands commitment, if it is to be understood. It deals with the way life is lived, not with theories about the nature of life. That is to say, God's word is always a word *to* us, never a word *about* us. It can never be regarded with passing interest; it always demands active appropriation. It is this word which meets man and summons him to decide for or against it, which summons him to historical existence rather than theoretical speculation.

Unfortunately, man normally lives in the world in such a way that he understands himself and his existence in terms of the world. He is thus imprisoned by that history and by that world, which bind him to themselves, and thus to the past. In Biblical language, this is what Paul means when he speaks of "living in the flesh," says Fuchs.[21] That also means that the course of history has been constituted by sinful men, and thus history in its variety of movements represents the works of sinful men. When Christ comes, therefore, and opens to man a new future, which offers man a present based on a future (love) rather than a past (sin), it means that Christ is the end of that history.[22]

The contrast Fuchs here points to, namely, between history constituted by the acts of sinful men and the future characterized by Christ's love, is nothing other than the contrast Paul was trying to make between law and gospel, so far as Fuchs is concerned. This differentiation plays a key role in Fuchs's theological thought. In this instance, law is equivalent to history, as gospel is to Christ, but this contrast is found throughout Fuchs's writings. In general, it would seem fair to say that for him, law deals with those aspects of man which reflect man's attempt to provide the basis of his existence for and by himself; law points to man in his self-assertion and in his desire to achieve security in the world. Gospel, on the other hand, deals with the abandonment of such efforts and the acceptance of the self as grounded in God, and thus living in faith. Such argumentation is fortified all through Fuchs's writings with a variety of exegetical attempts, some more ingenious than others. The important point to note here, however, is not the success of such exegesis but the intention to ground theology exegetically. It shows the intention of Fuchs's theological work.

As with the coming of the gospel, then, the power of the law is at an end, so with the coming of Christ, history is brought to an end. Not, of course, chronological history; year continues to follow year even after Christ has come. Rather, history is ended in the sense of history as the arena from and by which human existence is determined. That that is the case, Fuchs argues, is reflected in the fact that early Christian theology was characterized by a self-understanding divorced from all considerations of chronological history. If that is not the case with Paul, it must be remembered that Paul was, because of his past, an "outsider," and was also perceived to be such by the "brethren."[23] Early Christianity understood itself as a linguistic, not a historical, phenomenon. Unfortunately, the power of faith productive of new language was soon transformed into a power productive of a new interpretation of history, which could lead to disastrous results for faith.[24]

Chief among those results was the temptation to find security for the self in terms of the course history had taken, supposedly under God's direct guidance. Fuchs argues that the New Testament itself shows (e.g., Rom. 1:18 to 3:30) that man is denied any possibility of grounding his existence in history in that way. In fact, the intention of faith is to call into question all possibility of such self-assertion and security based on history.[25] All that history can do in any positive way is to cause man to ask about the real truth of faith, which clearly cannot be based on the course of history. And one of the most important insights of faith for the new hermeneutic is precisely the realization that man can find no security for the self in history. All history can do is reveal again and again the precariousness, the insecurity, the questionableness of human existence.[26]

There is another reason why faith cannot base itself on the course of history or on historic event. Faith, as we have seen, is related to the future in such a way that in its light, faith allows life to be lived in the present in a totally new way. Thus, faith has its reality in the present, in the way life is lived here and decisions are made now. History, on the other hand, is the very denial of the present. History is, says Fuchs, revolt against the present, because it despairs of the present, because it anticipates the future merely as a repetition of the past. History deals primarily with the dead.[27] Obviously, any faith preoccupied with history understood in such terms would hardly express a new way of living and of seeing life.

Yet that is just what preoccupation with *Heilsgeschichte* leads to, if *Heilsgeschichte* means that the inevitable course which history must run has been revealed in the past, so that all one has to do is confidently await its final unfolding. To do that is precisely to view the future as a mere repetition of the past. It is, in the eyes of the new hermeneutic, to find a security for the self in the past, which means to find it in precisely that place where finding security means losing the self as open to the future. Furthermore, to be able to find "objective facts of salvation" in history (i.e., events on the basis of which reality is altered, regardless of the self's decision regarding them) is to function on the basis of an understanding of time in which time has become man's "slave," since man knows the outcome already. In this view, time stands at man's disposal, something which, as we have seen, is the polar opposite of faith's understanding of time as a gift of God, to which man must be open. If the course of history is pre-determined, there is no true future, the self is determined by the past which has already happened, and the present is lost as a time of decision that allows the self to constitute itself as a self.[28] Any tendency toward such a view of the relationship of faith and history, finally, represents a perversion of the basic Christian faith. To accept such a view, Fuchs argues, means to pervert what is essential to a truly Christian view of the self and history.

Fundamentally, therefore, such a view of history, such *Heilsgeschichte*, Fuchs argues, is the result of speculative, Hellenistic thinking, and represents, in its attempt to tie everything together, a tendency, foreign to faith, toward the assertion of the self over all things. It is the attempt to gain security for the self on the basis of knowing what to expect in the future, since the shape of the future has been completely revealed in the past. Yet it is just such security that is the very opposite of faith. Rather than attempting to decipher the plan that history must of necessity follow, true faith remains open to the future. Instead of constructing a plan for time, faith seeks to make use of time as the gift of God, i.e., in works of love.[29] As a negative example, i.e., as an example of the improper way of understanding time, Fuchs cites the speech of the Hellenist Stephen before the Jews (Acts

7:2 ff.). This speech, Fuchs argues, represents the Hellenistic (and therefore non-Christian) tendency to find a total, coherent plan for history. By way of contrast, Fuchs mentions I Cor. 15:20a, where, he argues, Paul proclaims the correct understanding of time. All of this also indicates why, for the new hermeneutic, any apocalyptic speculation must be looked upon as an attempt to decipher a plan for history, and thus as a perversion of the true intention of the Christian faith. For that reason, Mark, ch. 13, for example, cannot conceivably have been spoken by Jesus, nor even represent Jesus' intention, since Jesus represents the true (Christian) self-understanding which is by definition opposed to such speculation about the final course of history.

There is yet another reason, moreover, why *Heilsgeschichte* is at odds with the Christian insight into the nature of time and history. That reason lies in the fact that *Heilsgeschichte* removes the paradox of faith, in a "not yet" (of fulfillment) and a "no longer" (of sin), a paradox that is expressed by Paul in terms of statements about what God has done (indicative) and what man must do (imperative). Such a tension is, Fuchs argues, dissolved in *Heilsgeschichte*, which, he feels, tends to put indicative and imperative into chronological sequence rather than in existential tension.[30] In the end, therefore, understanding faith in terms of *Heilsgeschichte* means that the temptation of history, namely, to validate faith in terms of historic event, has triumphed over the true understanding of faith. It is an attempt to prove the truth of faith on the basis of historical reality, an attempt that, however the proof is sought, rests ultimately in man's desire to provide for his own security in the world. Such a desire has already invaded certain of the New Testament writings, however, Fuchs asserts. The attempt to validate faith on the basis of historic event is already far along in the Synoptic Gospels, for example, and any attempt to use Old Testament proof texts, whether in the Synoptics, or in any other New Testament writings, is further evidence of the attempt to find some proof for the truth of faith. That attempt is combated by the Gospel of John, and most portions of the letters of Paul, and must continually be combated by those who would uphold the valid insight of primitive Christianity into the true nature of faith. Any such attempt to provide proof for the truth of faith is completely at odds, says Fuchs, with true faith.[31]

This explains the vehemence with which the new hermeneutic attacks all suggestions that the truth of faith could in any way be validated by an appeal to some prior truth or reality apart from faith itself. If one makes faith depend on some prior, non-historical reality, one robs faith of its participation in historic existence, i.e., the need to participate in history by making decisions concerning one's self and its relation to past, future, and present. Furthermore, if one seeks to validate faith with an appeal to some historic event or reality, one delivers, willingly or otherwise, the certainty that faith must have, in order to be faith, into the hands of historical skepticism. In either case, faith as the new hermeneutic understands it would be destroyed by the attempt to ground it in some reality outside of, and prior to, faith itself. For that reason, Fuchs can assert that the "pre-understanding of faith is located in the *nihil*," which he associates with *creatio ex nihilo*.[32] That is to say, the moment faith seeks to prove the truth of its content, or to validate its claims, by an appeal to something other than faith itself, it has destroyed itself as faith. For this reason, the new hermeneutic has accepted as a fundamental tenet Herrmann's dictum that the ground of faith and the content of faith are identical.[33] That is, the basis from which faith springs is as much a matter of faith as the content that faith affirms. Faith is not a response to something that lies outside the sphere of faith, as though one could find that basis historically or rationally and then build faith on that original "non-faith" reality. Jesus, or his resurrection, as the ground of faith is as inextricably related to faith as is Jesus as the content of faith. To put it another way, Jesus himself, who is acknowledged by faith as God's Son, is the only witness to himself. One cannot therefore step outside the realm of faith in order to prove the validity of the decision that constitutes faith.

There is nothing in Jesus of Nazareth that compels one inevitably to faith in him. Only for faith is Jesus inevitably the basis of faith.

Any attempt, therefore, that would seek to guarantee the truth or validity of faith in some event or experience that exists apart from faith is an act of unfaith. That must be affirmed, argue the proponents of the new hermeneutic, despite the New Testament witness to the risen Jesus, and Paul's assertions in I Cor., ch. 15. In fact, those resurrection appearances can become problematic for faith, since they can tempt one to see in them an "objective" basis for faith. That means inevitably that Paul has gotten side-tracked in his argument in I Cor., ch. 15, especially in vs. 12–19, where in the midst of an appeal for faith he lapses into statements of unfaith. In these verses, Fuchs asserts, Paul has fallen into an (overly polemical?) attempt to prove the validity of faith by appeal to some "objective" event that gives rise to faith, an event that, as the basis of faith, is itself based not on faith, but on eyewitness reports. Rather, argues Fuchs, a genuine resurrection appearance can occur only within the context of faith. Only because Paul had *already* been exposed to the power of the risen Lord in the form of the believing community (Fuchs cites Rom. 13:8–10 to substantiate this) could the risen Lord have appeared to him as well.[34] It is inconceivable to Fuchs that it could have happened any other way. Faith simply cannot be grounded in anything but faith itself.

It is precisely at this point that we can begin to see why language appears such an appropriate entity for such a view of faith. If historic event is thought to be the key, then the temptation is immediately at hand, as Paul demonstrated, to use such an event as a proof for the validity of faith itself. If, on the other hand, the important element is not the historic event as such, open as it is to historical investigation and skepticism, but rather the language that event called forth as response to it, language expressing a way of carrying on life in the light of that event, then that linguistic response becomes the key. And then it is possible to overcome the temptation to ground faith outside itself, since language preserves the insight, in a way a historical event cannot, that the content of faith and the ground of faith are identical. Thus, faith is best summoned forth, as a way of seeing life, and nourished as such, by the language of faith that reflects such a way of seeing life. In this instance, faith can arise unburdened by the temptation to prove its own validity by appealing to something outside itself.

Even with language, however, there has been a temptation to imagine that the word of God, or the language of faith, is some special kind of language, as though God's word were somehow qualitatively different from human language and could thus serve as an "objective" prop for faith. But to think that is to misunderstand the relationship between faith's language and normal language, as we have already seen above. Rather, there is only one language, the language of the world and its reality, and that is the language faith employs. What is new, however, is the fact that faith employs this language in a different way. Faith speaks in a different way about the world and time and man, so that even though the old words are used, they convey something new. But precisely because this newness appears in the form of ordinary language, there is nothing objectively different about the language of faith, or God's word, which would make it objectively discernible as such. Faith is still the key. God's word does not reveal itself as such in any objective or neutral way. The word of God is seen to be that only by faith. Only when God's word is met with faith is it received as God's word. Thus, word of God and faith are inseparable.[35]

Such a view of faith carries with it some very important consequences. For one thing, a person cannot discern God's word as a mere spectator, rather than as a participant. Faith means hearing the word of God addressed to us in our concrete lives. Only when we hear what God says *to us*, only when we ourselves understand ourselves as the ones to whom God's Kingdom is addressed, will faith become truly possible. Only when Jesus comes to speech *in us* will the power of the risen Lord, i.e., faith, become a reality, since faith, and that means the language of faith, is the presence of the risen Lord. Faith is the event of this Lordship of the Lord in the world.[36]

That in its turn means that man is and remains dependent on the event of the communication of God's grace. Thus man, taken for himself alone, has, and can have, nothing in history that could give him any sort of security for his own existence.[37] There is no support at all for faith save that communication of the event of grace, which is itself an event of grace. It is by the communication of the event of grace that grace comes to a man, so that he may now understand himself in the light of God's grace, in the light of the present as the time of God's love. And when man understands that, grace has become an event for him. It is easy to see, then, how it can be affirmed that faith lives from the language-gain which the communication of the event of grace in Jesus has injected into the language. Faith is the hearing of that language, and the shaping of the self around it, so that the self in turn can speak it to others. When that happens, the "word-event" of God's revelation of himself in Jesus has occurred.[38]

Faith is grounded, therefore, not in any historic event taken by itself, nor in any historical account of something that happened in the past. Rather, faith, if it is to remain faith (and that means, seeking no ground for itself outside of itself), relies on the language of grace for its substance and its sustenance.[39] That that must be the case is clear when one takes into account the fact that the goal of the self is to achieve true selfhood through understanding itself in the light of the present as the time of God's love. No historic event, communication of which was withheld, could in any way affect the way the self understands itself, and any attempt to prove faith in terms of some event or reality outside faith would simply provide the self with precisely the kind of security that would keep it from understanding itself as open to God's future. Such security would, on the contrary, simply confirm the self in thinking it had its security in the past.

The basis of this language of faith, then, is the language summoned forth as response to the event of Jesus and to his way of understanding man and the world. Jesus announced the present as the time of God's love, and thus challenged man to understand himself as dependent on God rather than himself or the world. This linguistic response on the part of Jesus, by which he brought faith to expression, from which faith must live and in the light of which faith must understand itself, is found in the texts of the Bible, more particularly the New Testament. And in that case, it is of utmost importance that these texts be approached rightly, so that the intention of their language be correctly understood. We must therefore turn now to an investigation of that problem.

8

The Approach to the Text

THE REAL PROBLEMS of interpretation do not become evident in a concrete way until the actual attempt is made to translate and interpret a specific text. The difficulty lies in the fact that in the nature of the case every translation must, to some extent at least, do violence to the original, if for no other reason than that language must be transformed into something other than it originally was, i.e., another language. But if it is necessary to translate, it is not sufficient "simply" to translate, and right there lie all the depths of the hermeneutical problem.[1] Put in most basic terms, the question centers in upon the task of getting the point "out" of the text (*exegesis*) without reading so much "into" it (*eis*egesis) that what is arrived at is a total distortion of the text's intention. If interpretation is to be interpretation, and not free composition, then such distortion, inevitable though it is because of translation, must be kept to a minimum. If that is to be accomplished, however, the interpreter must know something of the nature of the text with which he is dealing, as well as the nature of the interpretative task in general (the "hermeneutical circle"). Such knowledge in turn will aid in determining what method of interpretation to employ, and how that method is to be carried out. We must now investigate the way in which the new hermeneutic confronts, and solves, these problems. And since there is no substitute for interpretation itself, we will, finally, have to observe the actual formation of the interpretation of a specific passage from the New Testament.

We saw earlier that one of the key categories for the new hermeneutic is "language-event," i.e., the language summoned forth by an event as response to it. But there is more to a language-event than that. In any confrontation with reality, we bring with us a certain pre-understanding, shaped by the language we speak, and by our previous experience in our traffic with the world. It is this pre-understanding which allows us to make sense of our daily experiences, and to fit them into our ordered conception of our world. Yet it is also true that, on occasion, we confront situations for which our pre-understanding is not sufficient, with the result that, to a greater or lesser extent, depending on the event itself, our whole approach to events is changed. Some event confronts us, as, for example, in the occurrence of personal or national tragedy, which causes us to call into question the prior unity of experience and ideas we had achieved, which in turn made up our pre-understanding. We must then attempt to include this new experience in our total understanding of ourself and our world. We must reach some decision about how this adjustment is to be made, if we are ever again to be able to speak with any confidence about the way things are. For this reason, when a person speaks about his (ordered) world, his language is never simply the expression of a more or less random collection of ideas. Rather, his language is a reflection of those decisions by which prior expectation and actual event have been adjusted to one another. The ability of language to bring about such a unity of experience and prior conception is what is meant by "language-event." It follows, given such an understanding of language-event, that it also underlies the unity achieved between people in their common use of language, and in the agreements that can be achieved through its use. This situation, in which men seek adjustment to one another through language, also belongs to language-event. The term "language-event," therefore, refers to the power of language to bring about unity within a man, and between men.[2] It should not be surprising to learn, therefore, that language-event and love are closely related to one another, so that love is that quiet language-event in which unity expresses itself visibly; or that faith, as our decision that responds to God's prior decision in favor of love, also belongs within the sphere of language-event.[3]

In the light of all this, it is clear why Fuchs can assert that he understands the preaching of Jesus to be a language-event, since that preaching demanded of his listeners that they decide in what way they would include his proclamation into their own understanding of themselves and their world. They had to decide whether to accept what he said as true, and follow him, or reject it as false, and ignore, or actively oppose, him.[4] For this reason also, this language-event creates the language that becomes normative for faith. To put it another way, this language-event produces texts that become the text for faith, since they reflect a decision that affects the way a person understands himself and others. The New Testament text therefore owes its origin to the language-event of Jesus' proclamation, and as such, i.e., as reflecting language-event, represents a decision about the way life is to be understood and lived.[5]

All of that is, of course, important for the way we look at the New Testament text, for what we understand it to be, and how we approach it. It is clear, for example, that the New Testament does not intend to be a historical record in any modern sense of the word. To analyze the New Testament as though it were such a record can only result in distortion of its intention. Rather, the text intends to be proclaimed. It is meant to confront men with the decision as to whether or not they are willing to speak the language of faith, i.e., to let Jesus' relation to God become event in their lives as well. Unless the text confronts the hearer with the decision of faith, it has been distorted.[6] Paul, for example, was continually forced to correct himself, lest the very clarity of his proclamation cloud, or eliminate, faith as decision.[7] The earliest Christian proclamation, therefore, intended to summon forth a decision regarding man's situation before God, and in that way it functions as the text for all subsequent proclamation. Only when the text eventuates in proclamation, in a summons to decision about God in the light of Jesus, is the intention of the text served.

Surely it is important to know that the New Testament text contains, indeed itself is intended to be, proclamation. But if the interpretation of that ancient proclamation is to be carried on in such a way that it may become modern proclamation as well, it is necessary that that ancient proclamation, that New Testament text, be understood. Indeed, if it can be "understood" by modern man, then the task of interpreting it to modern men has already taken a long step forward. But if that text is to be understood in a valid way, it is necessary for us to know something about the way in which understanding comes about, particularly in relation to a written text, lest what we take to be an "understanding" of it turn out to be little more than mere distortion. How is the "understanding" of a "text" to be achieved?

It would be a mistake to assume, as we saw earlier, that there can be any such thing as purely "neutral" or "uninvolved" understanding. Unless one knows something of the subject matter treated in a text, he will not really understand that particular treatment. Any understanding therefore presumes some degree, at least of "pre-understanding," before it can take place. To put it another way, one must know the right question to ask a text, if any answer is to be forthcoming. A question about atomic physics, for example, will not be appropriate to address to an oration of Cicero. But there is more to it than that. The way the question is put is all-important, since the way the question is asked will determine the way the answer will be given.[8] If the question is badly put, therefore, the answer received from the text will be distorted, i.e., the true intention of the text will not come to light.

Any serious work with a text, i.e., any attempt to understand, to "question" a text, will result in a "dialogue" in which the question put to the text will continually be refined in the light of what the text reveals. This back and forth between questioner and text we have already met; it is the "hermeneutical circle." In such a situation, however, it soon becomes apparent that one's pre-understanding must be allowed to be corrected or the text simply cannot be understood.

An example may clarify the issue. Because the Synoptic Gospels contain records of incidents in Jesus' life, there was a time when it was thought possible to construct a biography of Jesus from such material. Armed with the pre-understanding that the Gospels do talk about the life of Jesus, scholars made an attempt to get the Gospels to answer questions about Jesus' life, i.e., its biographical details. It soon became apparent, however, that there are gaps in the evidence (e.g., his life between twelve and thirty years of age), and that the Synoptic Gospels do not agree in the details they do give, to say nothing of the totally different order of events in the Gospel of John. There are two alternatives: either construct from imagination the missing evidence, and discount some details in favor of others, or reformulate the question about what the Gospels intend to tell us about Jesus. That is, one can either force the available information into prior categories dictated by the need for biographical data or conclude that the Gospels give the data they do about Jesus with an intention other than providing biographical information as such. As the history of New Testament scholarship has shown over the past few decades, the nature of the Gospels forced scholars to give up the attempt to write a biography, and to ask about the Gospels as proclamation. In this way, the question with which scholars approached the text was reformulated in the light of what they found the text to be, and of their experience with the text in attempting to learn something the text did not intend to tell. This is one way in which, historically, the hermeneutical circle was at work in efforts to understand the text.

If, however, one is unwilling to change the way he approaches the text, if he persists in attempting to "master" a text by forcing it to answer a question put which is foreign to the intention of the text, the inevitable result is distortion. And this, of course, is precisely the problem with "objective knowledge." Unless such knowledge meets certain prior tests (e.g., it must be empirically verifiable, or compatible with some world view) it cannot be "objectively" true. Thus, the results of the questioning are forced into a pre-determined mold, with the result that understanding will inevitably be distorted. Only when one will allow the subject matter under investigation to correct such presuppositions can understanding occur. Understanding is thus inevitably circular, and where that fact is denied, understanding is not possible.

It is well to recall that the "hermeneutical circle," originally described in the philosophy of Martin Heidegger, is not a method of achieving understanding, which is perhaps superior to some other method. Rather, the hermeneutical circle is a structural element of all understanding, and where understanding does not proceed in this way, it will not occur. It is therefore not a question of whether or not to follow the hermeneutical circle in attempting to understand something. If understanding is to take place, there is no alternative. But understanding can be fostered if the circular nature of understanding is grasped, and then not thwarted.[9]

When we confront the New Testament text, therefore, we must be prepared to have our expectations concerning what it has to tell us called into question, and perhaps even changed. The alternative is to force the material contained in the text into a mold of our own making, and in that case, no understanding of what the text intends to tell us is possible.

Now that we have investigated the nature of the New Testament, and have recalled briefly the way understanding takes place, we are ready to look at the way the New Testament is to be understood and interpreted. We saw earlier that the text of the New Testament is not so much a record of historical events as it is a record of the earliest proclamation of the Christian faith. We saw further that it is the intention of that proclamation to place a man before the decision of faith. That is, the text challenges a person to see things in relation to God the way Jesus saw them, and to act accordingly. That means that the text intends to interpret *human existence* in a specific way, i.e., in the light of Jesus, and the way he interpreted it. That in turn will mean that the New Testament cannot be understood apart from categories that are related to human existence. Indeed, really to understand the proclamation, i.e., to confront the decision, one must allow one's own existence to be challenged. Interpretation, therefore, must take place in the interpreter himself, and in his life.[10]

Furthermore, it rapidly becomes apparent to anyone reading the New Testament that it speaks about a Lord who wants to become our Lord. It speaks about one who confronts us with the claim for our total allegiance. It is therefore immediately apparent, in the New Testament, that man is not the one who is capable of providing ultimate meaning or security for his own life, any more than he is originally responsible for its existence. Thus, the New Testament confirms what man knows from his own experience as a historical being, namely, the questionableness of human existence. It is this questionableness which is the focus of the New Testament message, but in such a way that all possibility of securing his own life on his own terms is taken from man. The text points to God as the basis of existence, and calls into question all human activity that is not in accord with that basis. To read the New Testament, therefore, means to learn that one is in competition with God for the lordship of one's life. The call of faith is precisely the call to abandon such self-assertion over against God.[11] In that way, the interpreter of the New Testament finds his own existence called into question, finds himself in competition with God, and hears the challenge to abandon his quest for self-security, and to rely on God, who is the true basis of his existence. The one who set out to interpret the New Testament finds instead that the New Testament is functioning as the interpreter of his own existence.

Any approach to the New Testament that prevents the hermeneutical circle from functioning in that way will obviously result in distortion of the intention of the text as proclamation and as challenge to a new understanding of existence. For that reason, it is necessary to be very careful how one attempts to interpret those elements of the New Testament which seem to speak of something else, e.g., cosmological descriptions or eschatological or apocalyptic speculations. Valid interpretation must seek to bring such discussions to bear on man's existence, which is their true point. That means New Testament interpretation, to be valid, must be "existential" (i.e., it must be related to man's existence) rather than, say, historical or cosmological. Existential interpretation thus seeks to bring such non-existential elements back to their proper focus, i.e., back to the question of human existence, and to the decision about how the self will understand itself in the light of the New Testament witness to Jesus.[12]

It is apparent that in this instance, the hermeneutical circle has functioned in the following way. One comes to the New Testament with a question, say, about the course history will follow in the future. One finds, however, that when the New Testament does speak about history, it constantly relates it to man, and puts to man the challenge of understanding himself within history as God's creature, and then acting appropriately. As a result, the pre-understanding with which the text is approached must be altered so that the question is framed in terms of man's existence. This altered pre-understanding is then termed "existential interpretation" because it asks questions about how man's existence is to be carried on in the light of the message of the New Testament.

The whole of existential interpretation (Bultmann, Fuchs, and others) thus represents an altered pre-understanding, i.e., altered from an earlier pre-understanding that sought to find answers to questions about history, e.g., when the world would end and what the course of history would be prior to its end. The suggestion, therefore, which has from time to time been advanced, that the new hermeneutic, or existentialist interpretation in general, change its pre-understanding regarding human existence in such a way as to take into account the historical or cosmological elements found in the text will be rejected as going back to a kind of pre-understanding inappropriate to the text. Pre-understanding does not change daily or weekly. Existential interpretation understands itself as working out the implications of a shift in pre-understanding that occurred sometime ago, and until those implications are worked out, it will be out of the question for them to alter that pre-understanding in any significant way.

It is therefore one intention, at least, of existential interpretation, to hinder interpretation of the New Testament from becoming merely the recovery of factual, or "objective," information. Rather, what existential interpretation, and therefore the new hermeneutic, is driving at is a decision related to concrete, individual life. The text is seen as requiring an "existentiell" decision. In using such terminology, Fuchs is making use of a distinction, made earlier by Bultmann, between "existentiell" and "existential." In this terminology, "existentiell" refers to those things related to concrete life, so that the "existentiell" decision for faith is the decision of a specific individual at a specific time and place to believe. As such, it is completely unique, and is intimately connected to one individual, concrete set of circumstances. Whenever a person makes the decision of faith, i.e., decides to meet some concrete event in the light of faith, he makes an "existentiell" decision. Obviously, such decisions are continually being made, and must be made, if the person is continually to achieve selfhood.

"Existential" on the other hand, refers to the structure of human nature that makes such a decision necessary and possible, if the self is to achieve true selfhood. Thus, an "existentiell" interpretation, i.e., the actual decision to believe, needs an "existential" interpretation, whose purpose it is to reflect on, and clarify, what is presumed, and acted on, in the existentiell interpretation. Otherwise, an existentiell interpretation may be led, in the heat of the moment, to make some rather poor decision in the name of faith. To find an answer from the Bible for a specific situation is an existentiell interpretation. To ask whether, and how, such an answer may legitimately be gained, is the task of existential interpretation. Existential interpretation cannot provide the answer to an existentiell situation; only the individual involved in it can do that. But existential interpretation can seek to relate the New Testament text to concerns of human existence, thus providing resources for those existentiell decisions.

In dealing with history, therefore, existential interpretation will not seek to recover merely factual information. Instead, it will seek to relate historical time to the concrete life of man.

Rather than dealing "with" historical time as such, existential interpretation, says Fuchs, is concrete interpretation of time, i.e., an indication of what it is now "time for." Putting it another way, one could say that existential interpretation analyzes the text in the light of the decision for which the text as proclamation is driving, namely, the decision to understand the present as the "time for" faith.[13]

How is such an interpretation to be carried out, or better, how are we to begin so that such an interpretation is the result? How do we approach the text, so that it functions correctly, i.e., in terms of human existence? To ask such a question is to ask about a "hermeneutical principle." By "hermeneutical principle," Fuchs, for example, means the principle by which, or the situation within which, understanding gets underway. It is a way of approaching the text, a way of questioning it, so that the text can be properly understood. Such a hermeneutical principle does not explain what understanding is or even tell what the correct understanding would be. Rather, it sets the desired process of understanding in motion. It creates the situation within which understanding can happen. For example, Fuchs says, if you want to understand what a cat is, put a mouse in front of it, and see what happens. The mouse is here the "hermeneutical principle" that sets the "catness" of the cat in motion. The mouse is that which causes the cat to show itself for what it is. It allows the cat to "happen" as cat.[14]

A hermeneutical principle is thus something that allows, or even forces, a text to "happen," i.e., to show itself, and its intention, for what it truly is.[15] The hermeneutical principle will be a way of approaching the text, or a question directed to the text, which will allow the text to say what it wants to say. Put another way, we may say that the hermeneutical principle will point to the "locus" of truth.[16] It will indicate where the truth of a text is to be found.

What, then, is the hermeneutical principle for the New Testament? Obviously, says Fuchs, the locus of truth in the New Testament is Christ, as the Pauline formula "in Christ" alone would be enough to show.[17] But that locus itself is in need of interpretation. What does "Christ" mean for us in the present situation? And what good would it do us to know truth were located "in Christ" if it could not affect us? No, the task of interpretation is not finished with that answer. The process of understanding the text, in fact, has not yet really got under way.

So, we must ask again, what is the "hermeneutical principle" for the New Testament? It is apparent, Fuchs argues, that the hermeneutical principle cannot presume the presence of faith in the interpreter. If that were the case, no such principle would be needed, since the text, whose intention it is to call to faith, would itself not be needed. As a matter of fact, the gospel itself does not presume the presence of faith for its understanding.[18] Otherwise, it could never be directed to unbelievers. Rather, the hermeneutical principle, which New Testament faith itself requires, must be neutral toward faith. What, then, is that principle? It is the question each man raises, and which, as a man, he must raise, namely, the question *about himself*. It is a question prompted by the estrangement from himself experienced by the sinner, which is deepened when he first hears the claim that God is his Lord. This is the question the New Testament presumes when it makes the assumption that everyone knows what guilt is. All of this points to the fact that the hermeneutical principle of the New Testament is the question about the self, prompted by the estrangement of the self from itself, an estrangement every man knows in terms of a gulf between him and his true self.[19]

It is this question which sets the process of understanding the New Testament text in motion. It is this question which allows the text to function as it intends to function: as an address to the self, not as information about some historical event or cosmological structure. This is the hermeneutical principle that allows the text to "happen," that allows it again to become a language-event. When that happens, those addressed by the text may respond by themselves learning the language of faith summoned forth by the language-event underlying the text, namely, Jesus and his proclamation. And when that language of faith is learned, man may respond to life, in faith, as did Jesus. In that way, the text itself, as language-event, may again become language-event for us.

If, however, the question about the self is the key to understanding the New Testament, then it means that the answer will also concern the self. We saw that the question shapes, and shares in, the answer. That is also true for the New Testament. Since the question concerns the self, so will the answer. And that will be its total content. In fact, Fuchs asserts, nothing more is said about us in Christ than we are able to comprehend within the question about the self.[20]

It is clear, as Fuchs notes, that with such a view of the meaning of Christ, the task of demythologizing the New Testament is decisively set forward, if not in fact solved. If one learns nothing in the New Testament about Christ that cannot be reduced fundamentally to something that bears on the man engaged in the question about his own existence, then there is no room left at all for "myth," if myth means information *about* something that is not involved in the question of the self. Such information, for example, as the date at which the world will end or in which heaven paradise is located. Faith in this view cannot consist in knowledge *about* some historic act, nor even in some confession, the saying and believing of which would guarantee entry into some future (mythological!) heaven. For Fuchs, as for Bultmann before him, existential interpretation of the Christian faith means faith has significance for the self in the world now, or it has no significance at all.

This is the sense, then, in which the hermeneutical principle gives the locus of the truth of the gospel. That locus is precisely in the question about the self, as it finds itself estranged from itself, burdened with guilt. It is a question that does not presume faith in the questioner, but a question that does open the way for the decision about the self contained in faith.[21] The question of the self, in short, is the existential condition, or concern, upon which interpretation depends.

But how does this work itself out in actual practice, in the actual exegesis of the text? What is the "existentiell" condition,[22] the attitude of the interpreter as he approaches the text? It is simply the honesty, or the moral seriousness, with which he confronts the text. If the interpreter honestly faces the text, and honestly attempts to understand it, the text will not forsake him. That is, if a man, who as a man is by that very reason involved with the question about the self, comes to the text honestly and seriously seeking an answer to the dilemma of the self, he will find an answer, simply because, as we have seen, the language of faith is precisely the language of existence that understands itself as the self it is.[23] Such an approach to the text allows room for the process of understanding to get under way, unblocked by any presuppositions about the text that will hinder it from answering the question about the self.

It is one thing to contemplate such a discussion of interpretation in the abstract, however; it is another to see it in actual operation. It is to this latter task that we must devote the remaining pages of this chapter, and, in a broader range, of the next. Let us begin with a passage that Fuchs himself chose to use to illustrate what he wants to say, namely, Phil. 2:6–11.

Fuchs begins with a translation of these verses. His translation may be rendered into English in the following way:[24]

> (6) He was in truth like God entire
>   Yet thought it as robbery to aspire
>   To be God's equal.
> (7) In sequel,
>   In order nothing for himself to save,
>   He chose to take the lot of slave
>   In human form.
> (7b) Though this offered him but to be like men,
> (8) He also suffered that as loss,
>   Obedient even as far as death,
>   Death on a cross.
> (9) For that God raised him to heights extreme
>   And gave to him the name supreme:
> (10) At that Jesus-word bow every knee
>   Above stars, on earth, within the sea!

> (11) And be no tongue that does not cry
>   Jesus Christ is *Lord!*
>   To honor the Father complete thereby.

Fuchs begins his interpretation by differentiating briefly between the three words *schēma* (v. 7b), *morphē* (vs. 6, 7) and *homoiōma* (v. 7), pointing the reader for more details to the appropriate articles in Kittel, *Theological Word-Book of the New Testament*. Since vs. 10–11 are reminiscent of Isa. 45:23, Fuchs argues, we will have to take the language of the Septuagint (the Greek translation of the Old Testament) into account.[25]

"We are thus reminded of Gen. 1:26 (with which Ps. 8:6 and Wisdom of Sirach 17:3 may be compared). If we further remember the phrase 'you will be like gods' in Gen. 3:5, we may paraphrase these latter words: 'you will not die!' Thus, 'being like God' is in the first instance a reference to God's power of life, which is the basis of his sovereign power as judge. God gave man a share in this power of judging, but not in his power of life. The phrase 'like God' in Phil. 2:6 refers, on the contrary, to the original sharing in God's power of life. The 'form of God' (v. 6), seen in contrast to the 'form of slave' (v. 7), refers, however, to the ruling power, which is of course bound up with a position above and beyond death. Verse 6 apparently has Gen. 3:4 ff. in mind. If one also recalls that in the Greek language, the 'form of slave' (*morphē doulou*) is equivalent to 'body' (*sōma*), then 'spirit' (*pneuma*), which also possesses power, can stand behind the phrase 'form of God' (*morphē theou*; 'spirit'—*pneuma*—is equivalent to 'glory'—*doxa*), if one takes customary Hellenistic linguistic usage into account. Of course, that is not expressly stated. Nor does it say that the preexistent One emptied himself of the spirit. He remains, in Pauline phraseology, the Son. To that also corresponds the obedience of Phil. 2:8, which is, as it were, only possible with the spirit. What he really empties himself of is the privilege of being free from death. But even that says too much, since death has power only over sinners (Rom. 5:12). Rather, he empties himself of any envisioning of that freedom, so that he becomes as a slave, and as a result he does not shy away from the resulting death, because he wants to take upon himself, wants to enter into, a human life that is determined solely by the will of God or that is becoming visible in a new way as such a life.

"Now it must become apparent which power in *truth* may be called the power *extra nos* (beyond ourselves): the power of cosmic death or the power of God. Because God stepped completely out of himself in his Son, he remains precisely power *extra nos*. In that way he becomes a power that impinges on us in a historical way, with the result that our *sphere* has become another through him. God 'in himself' would be nothing more for us.

"We must now take into account the word 'name' (*onoma*), which appears in the second portion of the passage, vs. 9–11. Being Lord belongs of course already to the 'form of God' of v. 6. But, he who was completely like God, did not (for that very reason) want to display himself equally as Lord, but rather, he desired (again, precisely *because* he was like God!) that the power of God, the Divine, should appear at the point where man no longer experienced this power as one that saves. He exposed himself to estrangement from God (which equals estrangement from life) in order that the divine power could come near redemptively to those who were estranged (cf. Isa. 45:22, *et al.*). The song sings of the redemptive dawn of the saving power of God in the Son's dark journey into death.

"And more! In this 'emptying' (*kenōsis*), it is precisely the 'image' (*eikōn=morphē theou*) of the Son which is completed as the self-emptying of love. Love's mystery consists in the fact that it rules in such a way as to free, in that it gives itself; that it elevates and saves, in that it humiliates and sacrifices itself; that it becomes visible only at the point where there is nothing more to see; that it illumines at the point where we surrender ourselves. Because and in that Jesus allowed himself to be determined as the revelation of God, the becoming visible of the Divine, even to the point of death, God allows us to experience the beginning of the power of love from Jesus' death. The power of death becomes in that way the medium (I could also have said, 'mirror') by which is made visible the power of divine love. For that reason Jesus, the one crucified, is to be praised as exalted by the confession of his name, and thus (also) to be exalted *in us*. Now we can understand that he humiliated himself *for our eyes*. The humiliation *for us* (which has already happened) corresponds to the (coming) exaltation of Jesus *in us*. Therefore, we are *first* asked whether we have *understood* Jesus' humiliation, and we are asked that, in that we are asked about our frame of mind (*phronein*), v. 5: whether we are all together intent upon exalting that Jesus in *us* who descended into death *for us*, i.e., intent upon praising him in the 'place of praising.' He who wants to see the light of the divine power of love rise to the heights must affirm the reality of death as the locus of its (love's) appearance. We can exalt Jesus in us only by being ready to expose ourselves to the distress of our existence. Here sin is the presupposition of grace, not in the sense that one must sin to receive grace, but rather in the sense that one can perceive grace only at the point at which one has been met as sinner by grace, namely, in the deadly abandonment of one to whom everything announces only that he is lost, *because* everything is lost."[26]

Following this commentary, Fuchs explains that he was seeking, in the translation, to imitate the liturgical force of the text, but that in his interpretation, he sought to get rid of the "playful" elements of that imitation. It is necessary, however, he asserts, in any interpretation, to establish a "mood," provided of course the mood of the interpretation is comparable to the note of truth struck in the text. Fuchs also explains that he introduced the word "sea" into v. 10, where the song reaches its climax ("within the sea"), so as to make clear that the "cry" of the afflicted in v. 11 is a cry of both desperation and jubilation. This, he argues, enables him to find the theme of death (those "within the sea," apparently) as central to the poem. This is a matter of considerable importance since, he goes on, given our state of affairs, it is apparently only by way of an "existentiell" understanding of death that we come to the point of being able to see the full truth of this passage. Only death unites both complaint and love, "since death speaks the language of complaint and mirrors the visage of love."[27] Only where the question of the self becomes serious (i.e., in facing death) can the language of the New Testament become meaningful. The question of the self, asked honestly and seriously is, as we saw, the hermeneutical principle of the New Testament. Only in the face of that question does the text really "happen."[28]

We have now seen an example of the way the application of the hermeneutical principle can "unlock" a text, force it to reveal its intention, and allow it to function as it ought. A poem that, on the face of it, seems to speak of some kind of metaphysical-historical events (Jesus, present with and equal to God, sheds that divinity to become man, dies obediently on a cross, and for that is then raised up to heaven, given God's name and accorded universal worship) is revealed, upon confrontation with the hermeneutical principle, to speak of the necessity of the self to admit that what happened to Jesus happened to inform and instruct us to abandon all security (i.e., admit we are sinners— so the import of the last few lines of the interpretation), and exalt Jesus, who willingly underwent humiliation in death for us. This exaltation of Jesus is our response to the language-event of Jesus, who, by his death, and therefore his love, showed us the way we too are to face, and respond to, life. Only by accepting death (having been so instructed in Jesus) as the place where love appears can we also experience God's grace and love. We find God only when we, in faith, abandon our self-secured selves to death, living out in our lives the way of life shown by Jesus in the way he lived out his.

Before we attempt any kind of evaluation of such a procedure, we must examine in more detail the kind of theological and exegetical results that it yields. We shall therefore devote our attention in the next chapter to examining the picture of Jesus, his activity and his significance, which emerges from the confrontation of the New Testament text with the hermeneutical principle.

9

The Figure of Jesus

PERHAPS NO JUSTIFICATION is needed for centering our attention on the figure of Jesus, as he is understood by the new hermeneutic, as the final area in which to investigate the results of the application of the hermeneutical principle (i.e., the question of the self) to the text. Surely he is the central figure in the New Testament writings, expressed or implied. Furthermore, a great deal of recent theology has been Christocentric, if not in the traditional use of the term, at least in the sense of being preoccupied with Jesus of Nazareth, often to the exclusion of other, traditional themes in theology. For such reasons it seems appropriate in this chapter to investigate the conclusions reached by the new hermeneutic concerning this central figure of the Christian faith.

When Jesus announced that the time of the Kingdom of God had come, he was speaking of an expectation, the Kingdom, which had exercised Jewish imagination long before, and which had recently been renewed by John the Baptist. What was unique in Jesus' announcement was the immediacy of that coming; *now* is the time of the Kingdom. But to be able to say that, Jesus must have understood the Kingdom in such a way that he himself was part of it. Here we touch a unique aspect of Jesus' relation to the Kingdom as far as the new hermeneutic is concerned: Jesus *understood* the Kingdom, and therefore could announce that it was at hand. Therefore, Jesus, in what he said and did, is simply the announcement of the presence of the (new) time of the Kingdom of God.[1] Further, if where the Kingdom is, there God is also, then Jesus, by recognizing and announcing the present as the time of that Kingdom, made God present for those who heard and saw him (Jesus). In Jesus, therefore, and especially in what he said, God was present in daily life.[2] It is therefore a mistake, argues Fuchs, to think of Jesus as an apocalypticist, awaiting the incursion of the Kingdom in some immediately future point of time. Such an expectation by Jesus would have crippled his proclamation of the presence of God *now*. Had Jesus really expected final redemption in the immediate future, therefore, in some apocalyptic sense, his preaching would have been robbed of its point.[3]

Jesus' relationship to the future must therefore be understood in a different way, namely, through his words, his language. Jesus' gift to his hearers is not insight into the future course of history, nor information about how or when it will end. Rather, his gift to them is his own words, formulated in such a way that the hearer has something to hold onto when troublesome times occur, something that can function as a model of faith for him.[4] In effect, therefore, Jesus' words prolong the time for decision that his coming introduced, the decision, namely, whether or not the present can be understood as the time of the Kingdom of God. But more, these words gave not only the time but the courage to believe. It was Jesus' language, then, that constitutes the way in which he would be effective also in the future.[5]

Jesus' authority is therefore manifested in his language, and what is important about him is to be found there. Any valid "history" of Jesus will of necessity have to be a history of his language, a language that, bestowed like gifts upon his hearers, prolongs for them—and for us!—the time to decide what time it is (i.e., the time of God's presence), and what it is time for (i.e., for faith). It is this language, and not some future cataclysmic event, which is capable of uniting sinners, and of uniting them in a way far beyond any possibility of unity that man could achieve. And the reason for that? Simply because in Jesus' words, language once again returns to its original function of displaying and promoting intimacy. If, as we saw earlier, language is the product of the intimacy, say, of family life, then one who could restore that intimacy to language would bestow upon those who used it the possibility once again of achieving such intimacy in daily life. To enter in upon Jesus' language, therefore, and to see the present as the time for God to work in the world, means to see in daily life the time for intimacy with God and with other men, as Jesus did.[6] Jesus thus restores intimacy to life, and unity among men, by providing a language of such unity and intimacy.

It is also clear, however, that man's life is not normally so characterized, apart from certain aspects of family life. Language has in fact been so distorted that its origin in, and function of, intimacy have been all but totally lost. Such distorted language causes us to live in a world of estrangement, suspicion, and hostility, not of peace, joy, and love. That can only mean that Jesus' language, which speaks of such a different world, either will seem incredible to us, or, on the other hand, should we believe what Jesus says, will make the world we know, and which seems obvious to us, questionable to a high degree. If the language of Jesus, speaking of the present time as time for the presence of God, now makes that presence available for us, then the situation mirrored in that language either will appear confused, or, if it is believed, will call into question the way the world had previously been understood. Such a disturbance of a person's conceptual unity by the introduction of language which is the response to a totally new situation, we noted earlier, is what is meant by a "language-event." Language, as we saw further, has the capacity to unite in a new way the impressions one has of his world, after the unity of the old conceptions has been destroyed. That means, therefore, that Jesus' proclamation is in fact a language-event, disturbing one's picture of the world, and challenging one to see the world in a new way.[7]

While all the words of Jesus have the capacity to function in that way, there is one type of saying that makes that capacity most clearly evidence, namely, the parables. We can gain our clearest insight into the nature of Jesus' words, therefore, if we look at them. Those parables, so characteristic of Jesus, and used so effectively by him, are apparently designed precisely to shed a new light on what before was considered obvious, challenging the hearer to take seriously this new way of seeing his world. Fuchs defines a parable as a kind of simile, "which tells of some individual event, not entirely typical, indeed, a border-line event, but a border-line event which is problematic."[8] It is designed to picture an event, seemingly typical, which nevertheless gives a glimpse of another "world," which seeks to disrupt the traditional way of looking at things. It gives a glimpse, therefore, of a familiar, yet strangely different world.[9] In so doing, the parable restores the character of action to language, by allowing language to seize reality, and to transform it into something new for the hearer or reader of that language. In the parable, the true function of language becomes transparent. The parable is thus language-event.[10]

Put another way, we could argue with Robert Funk that the parable seeks to expose the structure of human existence which is masked by custom and convention, so that a man may again understand himself for what he really is. The parable seeks to provide a new angle of vision, so that the strangeness of a new world, a new way of understanding things, may be perceived "through" the everydayness with which the parables deal. The parables lead to a world of familiar things that nevertheless are somehow, through that new way of looking at them, radically different. God, man, neighbor, ethical responsibility, personal involvement—all are familiar, yet strangely new in the parables of Jesus, when they are looked at from this new perspective which the parables illustrate.[11]

The parable, as language-event, thus gives us an example, a pattern for this new way of seeing the world. But by showing us how to see our world in a new way, the parable confronts us with the necessity either of choosing to live in terms of that new world or of refusing it in favor of the old world. The parable thus poses a choice between these two worlds, the world with which a man is so familiar that he fails to see the true situation vis-à-vis God and his fellowman or the parabolic world in which that very everydayness is transformed into a whole new way of seeing, and acting in, that same world. It is with that kind of decision that the parable is intended to present us.[12]

The parable is therefore an analogy to the kind of position one must take in relation to the truth which Jesus announces, namely, that the *present* is in fact the time of the Kingdom of God, and that life must therefore be transformed in its light. But we must be clear: the parable is not an analogy of the truth of the Kingdom as such. The parables are not a hidden description of the nature of God's Kingdom. Rather, they are an analogy to the *position* one is to assume when confronted with that truth. The reason for that is clear: the event of which the parables speak demands that man participate in its reality, not merely observe it, at a distance, as some new "objective" "fact." The parable is meant to draw the hearer into its situation as participant, so that he may make the decision with which the present as the time of God's presence confronts him. For that reason we can say that the parable is an analogy to a position regarding the truth of Jesus' proclamation, not an analogy of that truth itself.[13] The parables reflect the way Jesus understood the present, and the way he himself reacted to it. The parables, growing out of Jesus' understanding of God's Kingdom, and its coming into the present, thus show how one must act, what one must see, in the light of the Kingdom. The parables are a way of looking at life, not definitions of the nature of God's Kingdom.

While participation in the parable in the form of decision is required by the parable, however, what that specific decision is to be in any specific case is not defined. The parable, like any good metaphor, remains temporally open-ended. That is to say, it is able to perform its function of illuminating the world even when the world from which it draws its imagery is no longer, in detail, the contemporary world of the reader. Thus, how the parable is to be applied, i.e., what decision it requires concretely, is not itself a part of the parable. For that reason, the application of the parable to my concrete situation may not be immediately apparent. If, for example, the parable were intended to illustrate a universal moral truth, so that wherever or whenever it was told, its application would remain the same, then, once that truth were learned, the parable itself would no longer be necessary.[14] But then the parable would have forfeited its role of inviting participation in judgment on the situation pictured, and thus on the judger's own concrete situation. For that reason, Fuchs argues that the points of the parables are not defined in detail by the parable itself. Rather, so that the hearer may find its application in his own life, the point the parables make is quite broad. He gives the following interpretations of parables, among others: Mark 4:3–9: only at the end can one gather; Luke 13:6–9: patience sees success; Luke 14:16–24: familiarity breeds contempt; Matt. 20:2–15: goodness teaches love; Matt. 18:23–34: lack of mercy blinds.[15]

In the light of such a meaning attributed to the parables, it is clear that each individual person must decide, in the light of his own concrete situation, in what way the parable confronts him. Only in this way can the parable function as language-event, illuminating in a new way everyday life, and drawing the one who hears or reads the parable into a decision about how he will react to that "new" world.

The parables, therefore, show us the way in which Jesus understood his situation vis-à-vis the present as the time of God's presence, and that means they show us the kind of existence for which we must decide, and within which we are then to move. In the parable, the imminence of the rule of God is expressed concretely, and that means, in the language of everydayness. In this way the parable itself, by its language, points to the unity of present (everydayness) and future (God's Kingdom) to which Jesus' proclamation points. But the very analogical nature of the parable makes clear that what Jesus is speaking about is a particular way for existence to happen, to be lived. Thus, argue the proponents of the new hermeneutic, the parable calls the hearer to decide for Jesus' understanding of time, for his understanding of the new situation into which man and world have been placed because "now" is the time of God's rule.[16] Man is thus invited to understand himself in a completely new way, namely, as a man who can, in the "now" of God's presence, even love his enemies. To understand, and follow, the world of Jesus' parables means, therefore, to be able to call upon God as Jesus did. When that happens, Jesus' proclamation has truly functioned as language-event.[17] With such a view of the parables, it is clear why Fuchs can assert that it is Jesus' parables which, resisting death, lead to eternal life.[18] What he means by that will be clearer after we have seen his view of the meaning of cross and resurrection.

It is clear from the New Testament, however, that Jesus did more than just speak. The Gospels have much to record about what he did, and much of that is concerned with wondrous events. There is, however, little, if any, positive discussion of the "miracles" of Jesus within the writings of those who carry on the new hermeneutic. The reports of such mighty acts are apparently regarded as purely mythological in concept, and may apparently simply be ignored. The teachings are accorded much more respect than such activity reported of Jesus.

There is one event in Jesus' life, however, to which the theologians working within the frame of reference of the new hermeneutic have devoted a great deal of attention. That event is Jesus' death on the cross. According to the Gospels and Paul, as well as the rest of the New Testament, the events surrounding Jesus' death, and his rising again to life, represent the climax of Jesus' career. We must therefore see what meaning these events have within the perspective of the new hermeneutic.

It must be admitted, as Ebeling asserts, that from the beginning, the church has proclaimed that the Christian faith stands or falls with the witness to the resurrection of Jesus from the dead.[19] But to understand what sense that may have for the new hermeneutic, we must ask precisely what they understand "resurrection" to mean. It cannot refer to any event that could be verifiable apart from faith, nor can it be any "objective" event that could be perceived apart from faith. To speak of the resurrection in such terms is to speak mythologically, and thus to miss the point of the witness to those "resurrection events." We have already seen that the resurrection appearances of Jesus can function as a hindrance to faith. That means that reports of those appearances which can function in that way, such as those contained in I Cor. 15:5–8, must give way to the "truth of faith."[20] It goes without saying that what is true of the resurrection appearances would also be true of the stories of the empty tomb. Such traditions virtually guarantee that the resurrection will be understood mythologically, i.e., in some "objective" sense. Fuchs even suggests that the footrace between Peter and the beloved disciple, recorded in the Gospel of John, may in fact be intended to ridicule the whole idea of an "empty tomb."[21]

As is the case with everything else in the New Testament, the resurrection appearances, to be understood, must be seen in the light of the absolute priority of faith. Faith is necessary, and must be present, before those appearances can be understood. Apart from the experience of faith in the community of the faithful, Fuchs insists, the primitive community would have had no idea how to handle the witness to Jesus' resurrection. That in turn means that those appearances cannot be the basis of faith. Faith does not grow out of the resurrection; rather, the resurrection grows out of the cross, if one wants to use such terminology. The resurrection has no priority, either over the cross or over faith. Rather, faith in the cross as the saving act of God is the parallel, not the result, of the resurrection of Christ.[22] As a matter of fact, the resurrection appearances can be interpreted as a desire to control the future, rather than allow it to come from God. Those appearances, Fuchs urges, may well represent the desire to hinder the hoped-for future (i.e., "hoped for" in Jewish, apocalyptic terms) from dissolving, and that kind of attempt to shape one's own future, in one's own terms, Jesus himself had warned against in Mark 8:35.[23] To do that would be nothing other than to impose an alien "pre-understanding" on the events of the last days of Jesus.

The proclamation of the resurrection, truly understood, is therefore not the announcement of Jesus appearing risen from the dead in some "objective" (i.e., objectively ascertainable) way. Rather, the true proclamation of the resurrection is the proclamation of the scandal of the cross, a scandal that must repeatedly be overcome.[24] That scandal consists in the question whether God was as present in Jesus' cross as Jesus had claimed He was present in his life. To answer that question in the affirmative, i.e., to believe not despite the cross but *because* of the cross, means to confess the resurrection of Jesus. "Easter faith" therefore means simply to believe that Jesus was God's word to us; to believe that with Jesus, the time for God's word had come, and that thus Jesus was in fact that word.[25] Faith in the risen Christ therefore means the faith that the historical Jesus was God's word to us, and that that word was present, and is to be believed as present, in the very death of Jesus on the cross.

The power of the resurrection, therefore, consists in the comfort of the cross, the comfort, namely, of knowing that the one who was crucified possessed and possesses the power to transform and send forth his followers with the message of the cross to all men. Thus Jesus himself, the Crucified One, has the power to speak to us through this cross, and to say to us that he knows our weakness, and for that reason is our strength. And because he knows our weakness, he can be a comfort for us in the failure of our own Christian lives. The point of the earliest confession to Jesus' resurrection, or exaltation, consisted in the certainty that Jesus had undergone, and overcome, the tribulation under which all men live. The victory of the resurrection consists, therefore, concretely, in the victory of the words of Jesus over the death of Jesus on the cross. And this is precisely what Jesus had intended, Fuchs argues, as is shown in the way he formulated his sayings, and especially his parables.[26] If, then, the power of the resurrection consists precisely in the fact that the cross is proclaimed as comfort and succor, then to try to turn the resurrection into some sort of "objective" fact would be to rob men of the comfort of the cross. If the resurrection is

anything more than the expression of the power of that comfort, then the cross would be robbed of its comfort for us which
we need in the face of the failure of our own Christian existence.[27]

All of this is not to deny the importance of the appearances
of Jesus as the Risen One. But they are important, not because
in some (mythological) way they prove that Jesus is a divine
being, or because they verify objectively (i.e., in a way that can
be perceived apart from faith) that Jesus is victor over death,
but rather because they once again set in motion the eschatological proclamation of Jesus.[28] "Eschatological" here, of course,
does not refer to certain "objective" events (i.e., discernible
apart from faith), nor to events within history with which history ends. Rather, "eschatological" is used the way Bultmann
used it, i.e., to mean a proclamation that man can be free of
the past and of himself by accepting Jesus' appeal to abandon
the assertion of the self, and by opening the self to God's future. In this way, the sinful past loses its power to dominate the
individual, and as a result, the individual is "free" from that past,
and thus from history. For such a man, "history" as sinful past
has ceased as the dominant influence in his life. Eschatological
existence, as existence free from the domination of (sinful)
history, is possible in the life of faith, and this is the eschatological proclamation that was taken up again with the appearances of the risen Jesus.

The content of that proclamation, however, was immediately
determined and clarified by Jesus' cross, so that the Crucified
One became the content of the word whose proclamation the
resurrection appearances had set in motion. This proclamation,
as the language of God's presence with Jesus, means that the
language of God is the language of death that overcomes death.[29]
But this language of God has, in Jesus' cross, now become precisely the language of Jesus' cross. Thus the Crucified One has
been transformed into the word of the cross, the language of
God, which permits men to have faith in God as God *for* them.
In the language of the cross, the language of God has become
comfort and love for all men. This language of the cross means,

further, that men need never become speechless in faith, and
will never be left without help in time of tempting attacks on
faith. That help will always be present in the form of precisely
that "language of the cross." In the language-history of Jesus,
therefore, the event of the resurrection, i.e., Jesus' overcoming
death and remaining God's word to and for us, continues.[30]

But what does all of this mean in the light of the hermeneutical principle, i.e., the question about the self? What will happen
to the "text," whose meaning we have up to this point been
discussing, when the hermeneutical principle is juxtaposed to
it, so that the text may "happen"? The answer is rather clear.
In the light of the question of the self, the cross of Jesus means,
in simplest terms, that Jesus opposed the self-assertion of men
who feel compelled to ground and justify their existence for and
to themselves, and that he died as the final act of that opposition.

That means, then, that Jesus' cross is a judgment on our own
self-centered and self-assertive existence. The scandal of the cross
consists precisely in this judgmental aspect with which it confronts our lives. The cross represents the question whether or
not we are willing to let the crucifixion of Jesus function as
judgment on us. Jesus who died on the cross becomes historically
a question addressed to all men, the question whether they are
willing to allow Jesus to tell them that the time for freedom
from the necessity of self-assertion has dawned, a freedom which
has always existed as a possibility for men, and which for that
reason can readily be understood by them. With Jesus, this
possibility now takes on new reality, however, since in the cross
of Jesus, this freedom from self-assertion became event.[31] Hence,
even though that possibility of living a life free from the force
of self-assertion at the expense of others has always been a
possibility (in common parlance, a "theoretical" possibility), it
was a future possibility only. It had not yet become a historical
possibility in the sense that it had not yet become an event,
which carried with it the power of the word of God.

It is one thing for the possibility of selfhood free from self-
assertion to have become event in Christ; such existence of the
self free from compulsive self-assertion is also known as a future

possibility to philosophy.[32] It is another thing, however, to have this possibility of selfhood free from domination by self as a possibility *for me*. That is possible only in faith, namely, in the decision that that selfhood free from self (i.e., selfhood in love), which became event in the cross of Jesus, is the kind of selfhood which will become event *in me*. To accept the cross of Jesus as an event *for me* is the decision of faith that makes it possible for a selfhood in love to become present reality in me.

If such selfhood is based on a decision to let it be selfhood for me, then it must also be true, Fuchs argues, that at some point Jesus must also have come to the decision that a selfhood free from self-assertion was also the kind of selfhood he would lead. That is, Jesus himself must have decided that selfhood based on faith in God was the kind of selfhood he himself must live, even if that kind of decision led to suffering and death. That would mean, then, that to decide for faith, i.e., to decide to abandon self-assertion, would be a repetition of Jesus' decision to live that kind of life, even to the point of suffering. That also explains, incidentally, why faith can never be separated from suffering.[33] Jesus, the one who was willing to renounce self-assertion even to the point of death, is therefore the standard for, the model of, faith.

All of this can be summarized with the assertion that what God had in mind for man, he revealed in Jesus. Jesus is therefore not only the model for faith, he is in fact the model for man as man, i.e., as one who lets God be his God, and who thus lives as one having a future freed from the deadly necessity for self-assertion which bound him in the past. In that way, he accepts the possibility of truly becoming a self.[34]

This is also of significance in another way, however. What we have here is nothing less than a standard by which to measure the authenticity of the sayings of Jesus contained in the Gospels. Since Jesus is man as man ought to be, then everything he says will also have to be applicable to him as well as to other men. As a consequence, any word reported spoken by Jesus which would, or could, exclude him from its meaning or application must be excluded from consideration as authentic.[35] With such a criterion, the possibility of reopening the quest of the historical Jesus is given. But that quest is more than just possible. It is made necessary by the fact that Jesus is the model for our faith, which means we must repeat the decision for selfhood in reliance on God and his future which Jesus himself made. Our faith therefore demands that we recover as much of Jesus' expression of his faith as we can, purified from any distorting interpretations added by the later community.

We have, however, not said all there is to say when we affirm that we must see in Jesus the model of faith, or when we agree that we must believe as Jesus believed. That is true enough, but it must also be said that our faith depends on the words, the language, which Jesus' faith itself brought forth. It is his faith that brought forth the language that awakens and confirms our faith. The historical Jesus is therefore the linguistic event which is the ground of the event of faith. For that reason, we must assert that Jesus is both the witness to, and the ground of, faith. Jesus, by his language, points to the faith (witness) of which he himself is, as originator of that language, the source (ground.)[36] Therefore, the announcement of that faith, i.e., Christian proclamation, must lead the listener to the decision whether he is at one with Jesus in speaking the language of faith as Jesus spoke it. That in its turn means to presume, in such language, that man exists as man before God, as Jesus did, and thus make Jesus' relation to God an event for us as well. Faith can only understand what has its basis in Jesus, and what reflects his faith, and therefore such proclamation, as all Christian language, tests the extent to which we are in agreement with Jesus.[37] Only in that way have we any assurance that our faith has its witness and ground in Jesus.

That this is the case, Fuchs affirms, can clearly be seen in the theology of Paul. His letters make clear that Paul seeks to lead the believers into the language of the *cross* of Christ, which is the language of the decision to abandon the self and the world, a decision forced upon them by the self-judgment which Christ's cross brings about. That this is important for the community of faith is shown by the fact that Jesus unifies, not by seeking his own advantage, but by allowing others to matter, and to matter enough that he is willing even to sacrifice himself.[38] This same general point, Fuchs says, also underlies Paul's contrast between Adam and Christ. Adam's sin consisted in his forgetting that he was a being who was to remain open to the future, i.e., a being who had the task of understanding himself as the "reality of a possibility" (Fuchs's words). Instead, Adam asserted himself, tied himself to himself, and thus became bound to the past of that self, i.e., he understood himself not as living from future possibility but from past reality. In Jesus, this possibility of selfhood in reliance on God, and thus on the future, was repeated, thus making that possibility a reality once more. Thus, the self tied to sin and the past (Adam) now has as its reality the possibility of being open to the future as the time of God's grace (Christ). Jesus desired nothing for himself, as Adam had desired all for himself. With Jesus, therefore, the possibility of selfhood before God again becomes reality.[39]

It is clear then that the purpose of Jesus, and his importance for us, consist in his freeing man from all necessity of self-assertion or self-justification. We can say, therefore, that in the events surrounding Jesus of Nazareth, a decisive change in the history of human self-interpretation, of man's self-understanding, has taken place. Man now has the chance to be free from himself, because Jesus' words give man entry into Jesus' own joyful dependence on God. When Jesus brings this joyful dependence to expression in his word and parables, he is offering his hearers the possibility of a new self-understanding, namely, understanding the self as being in (joyful) relation to God. When Jesus does this, he brings God to speech (language), an event that restores to man a possibility to which he had previously been closed, namely, the possibility of understanding himself as the being under God that he always has been.[40]

When Jesus announces the need for such self-surrender, he reflects the status of man vis-à-vis God, Fuchs argues. "God," says Fuchs, is the absolute precondition to what man is. That is, God is the one who represents the limit on man so that man cannot be or become just anything he might want to. Naïvely to assert the self, therefore, means it is impossible to know God, since in that case, the self is occupying the place only God may occupy. To know God, and thus to live as man, such self-assertion must obviously be abandoned.[41] What Jesus desires, therefore, when he brings God to speech, is man's self-surrender, namely, the surrender of the self as a self bound to assert itself.

This self-abandonment which is required by Jesus, and the reality of whose possibility he himself represents, can also be expressed in terms of abandoning all attempts to exercise control over time, which is the ground, the origin, of existence. Rather than seeking to exercise control over time by understanding the present only in the light of what has happened in the past, which stands at man's disposal, one must rather open himself to the (unknown) future which is accepted as a gift of God. By allowing the present to be seen in the light of the future rather than the past, man thus abandons his attempt to exercise control over the present by seeing it only in terms of what he knows of the past. Jesus makes this possible by announcing the present as the time for God's rule, thus bringing the future as the time of God's love into the present. Man may then abandon the past, in terms of which he sought to assert and justify himself, and open himself to the present as the time for love, which means abandoning self-assertion and allowing others room for their existence as well.

By way of summary, then, we may say that inauthentic existence is life under the compulsion of self-assertion. Authentic existence, on the contrary, is knowing that the present, in the light of the future, is the time for existence in love. This means quite clearly that the way of faith is the way of love, and that faith in Jesus therefore means letting such love hold sway as God's work. The time Jesus announced is thus the time for love to prevail among men.[42]

In the historical Jesus, then, the One (God) who summons to

live has become a historical word to us, in that he announces that he is *for* us, in all his Godhood and majesty, and that that is the truth of our existence. What Jesus has done is to give us the language that enables us to understand ourselves in the light of that truth, thus bringing it about that the reality of God as the reality of love becomes the possibility of our own existence. Therefore, God as love becomes concrete in the language of love, which is the language of faith, whose ground and witness is Jesus of Nazareth.[43]

Nor should it be regarded as mere happenstance that love, language, and God thus converge in Jesus of Nazareth. If it is recalled that for Fuchs, the essence of language is permission,[44] and that as a result, language-event may be defined as an event in which such permission is granted (which is the essence of love), then it is not hard to understand why he can affirm that the new hermeneutic, in finding the meaning of Jesus to lie in the fact that he speaks the language of faith, and thus of love, is doing nothing other than following the inner tendency of language itself. In fact, he argues, that inner tendency comes to clearest expression in Jesus of Nazareth, and therein lies his greatness.[45] Thus, Jesus' language is language functioning as it is intended to function, just as self-understanding based on that language is the self functioning as it is intended to function, i.e., as self-under-God. It is not surprising that language is therefore seen as the key to understanding the Christian faith, since they have so much in common.

These, then, are the results of allowing the text to "happen" by applying as hermeneutical principle the question about the self. There are many points that have come up in the course of this discussion upon which comment could be made. We will look at some of those points in our final chapter.

10

Reflections on the New Hermeneutic

THERE IS MUCH that can be said about the new hermeneutic, both for and against, in a variety of areas: the view of language, the dependence on the Heideggerian approach to philosophy, and the hermeneutical principle which is chosen and the way it is applied to the text, to mention but a few. Obviously we cannot discuss all of them in this final chapter. Let us therefore attempt to survey the basic positions occupied by the new hermeneutic, and seek to show, in the course of such a survey, where some of the strengths and weaknesses may lie in this way of doing theology.

Let us begin with the basic stance of the new hermeneutic with regard to man.[1] In accordance with the Heideggerian analysis, it is held that man is a being who is constituted by his relationship to himself. That is, how a man functions will be determined by this relationship to himself, which is expressed in the way he understands himself. The key element in human "nature" is thus this self-understanding, which will determine how man reacts to life, to his world, and to his fellowmen. That will have as a consequence that the only way a man can be changed in any significant way is through a change in the way he understands himself. A change in self-understanding will mean a change in the way man faces his life and his world; indeed, it will mean a change in the very shape of the self, since the understanding relationship to the self is what constitutes man as man.

Of all possible ways to understand oneself, however, only those are of any real value that are true possibilities of self-understanding. That is, unless a self-understanding has in fact proved capable of actualization in history, it cannot be taken seriously as a possible self-understanding for any man who lives as a historical entity. Therefore, if the Christian faith is to have any effect on man, on his life, it will have to be in terms of offering a man a self-understanding that has in fact proved its validity by having been actualized by a man in history. Otherwise, the Christian faith will remain unrelated to historical existence as a way of self-understanding, and will not really be able to exert any kind of self-shaping, life-altering force.

That the Christian faith is in fact a viable alternative for the self-understanding of historical man is shown by the fact that it was actualized, in history, by Jesus of Nazareth. But it is only in those terms that the Christian faith can have validity. No doctrine about Jesus as representative man, effecting a change in human nature understood as a metaphysical entity, in which all men share, can affect a self whose only "nature" is its relationship to itself. Thus, only what Jesus can have actualized as a historical man can have any validity as a possible way for historical man to understand himself. This is, of course, the point of Bultmann's program of demythologizing, which the new hermeneutic has accepted as a valid task and goal.

The theological problem, therefore—and at this point the real theological work of the new hermeneutic begins—is to get at Jesus' own self-understanding. If that can be recovered, we will have a valid model for our self-understanding, since it is a self-understanding that has been actualized in history, thus proving itself a real possibility for any man. It is also true, however, that the way in which any man comes to terms with himself and with his world is by means of language. Language is man's reaction to life, and the medium by means of which he achieves understanding and lucidity about himself and his world. Language is essential not only to communicate such an understanding; it is essential to arrive at any such understanding. That means that what one thinks of life, and of his relationship to it, will be expressed in his linguistic response to life.

The way to get at Jesus' understanding of, and reaction to, life will therefore be by recovery of his language, in which that understanding came to expression, and thus to clarity, both for himself, and for others. But a great deal is reported about Jesus in the New Testament, both of what he said and did. How can we determine what is of value for us now? The working criterion is simply the application of what has been said about any self-understanding, namely that it must be possible for man if it is to be valuable for him. That is, the working criterion for understanding, and interpreting, Jesus, to ourselves and to men of our time, will be: Does the event, or the language, reported of Jesus, reflect a self-understanding that is possible for man as he must live in history, and within its limitations?

This criterion works itself out in the material the new hermeneutic finds valuable, and the material that is ignored. The parables, for example, where they can be understood as the reflection of a way of reacting to life, will be very valuable. The insights that such an approach to the parables is able to provide surely constitute one of the major contributions of the new hermeneutic. This approach solves a basic problem concerning the parables, namely, Why, if the parables are supposed to be descriptive of some reality independent of the language itself, i.e., the Kingdom of God, did Jesus not simply make clear, descriptive statements about what that Kingdom was like? Why "dress up" that information with parables? The answer that a story is better remembered than a teaching is belied by the fact that many teachings not in story form were in fact remembered, and it is made even less convincing by the recollection contained in the Gospels themselves that the parables were a source of confusion as well as clarity. If, on the other hand, the parables are stories meant to illustrate a way of reacting to life, then how could that reaction be communicated in any other way than by stories dealing with events in life, and showing, in paradigmatic form, what that reaction to certain kinds of events ought to be?

The value of the parables lies in recognizing in them a way of reacting to life, rather than seeing them as (puzzling or poetic) descriptions of the contours of the Kingdom of God. Much fruitful theological work remains to be accomplished in spelling out the consequences of this way of approaching the parables.

Miracles, on the other hand, are best ignored in this approach. No self-understanding that presumes the ability to work miracles will do historic man any good, since he is simply not that sort of person. The miracles are best accounted for, if Jesus is to be preserved as a valid model of possible self-understanding for me, as later intrusions into the tradition about Jesus, motivated by the desire to have Jesus be as effective a miracle worker as any other figure who was highly esteemed by the Hellenistic world. It is not accidental that reports of the miracles of Jesus occupy no place in the discussions of the new hermeneutic.

The need to find in Jesus a possible model for the self-understanding of historic man also explains the difference, it would appear, in the treatment accorded to the traditions about the cross, and the resurrection of Jesus. The cross is still valid for consideration, since it can represent the way Jesus understood himself in relationship to life. It can illustrate how he thought he must react in the circumstances in which he found (placed?) himself. The way a person chooses to die can say a great deal about the way he understands himself, and about the way he understands, and reacts to, life. The resurrection, on the other hand, cannot be interpreted in any way as reflecting Jesus' own self-understanding. It is not something he did, it is something that happened to him. And it happened to him after it was no longer possible for him to do anything, i.e., after his death. The resurrection cannot, therefore, reflect Jesus' reaction to life, and cannot, as a result, represent a possible way for man to understand himself. The only way to find meaning in the resurrection is to relate it to the cross, indeed, to absorb its meaning into the meaning of the cross. That is, of course, what happens in the new hermeneutic.

This leads to two problems, however. The first consists in the fact that the resurrection has traditionally been regarded as Jesus' victory over death, and God's vindication of his claims and his mission from the charges of his enemies. If the resurrection cannot be understood as that victory, where are we to find anything but defeat in Jesus' death at the hands of those who opposed him? The answer is found in the relationship of love to the cross. "Love" is defined as allowing another "room" in which to live by abandoning the kind of self-assertion in which the self seeks its own life at the expense of others. If one were willing to die rather than abandon the abandonment of self-assertion, that death would be a victory for such an abandonment of self-assertion, or, in other terms, a victory for love. Jesus' cross can thus be understood as showing his willingness to abandon self-assertion even if it meant death, and the self-understanding that led to that act shows itself superior to death by valuing such a way of meeting life even more than it valued life itself. The cross can then be regarded as the victory of Jesus' way of meeting life, i.e., in love, even over death itself. It is such an approach to life that is then described by the word "faith." Faith is to see life, and meet it, in terms of Jesus' victory over death through love.

The second problem with this way of understanding the resurrection lies in the fact that this is obviously not the way the early church, as reflected in many parts of the New Testament, understood it. Much of the early church, to judge by the New Testament, understood the resurrection as evidence that God was at work in history to vindicate Jesus and to bring about his Kingdom in the very near future. Instead of seeing the resurrection as pointing to the cross as the capstone of a way of facing life, the early church saw the resurrection as historical evidence that God was actively at work within history. But if such a way of viewing the resurrection was counter to Jesus' own understanding of his mission as understood by the new hermeneutic, i.e., a mission of proclaiming a way of facing life rather than announcing a series of apocalyptic events, how could the (later) authors of the New Testament writings have come to view the resurrection, and thus the purpose of Jesus, so differently? Fuchs finds the answer to that, it would appear, in terms of Heidegger's understanding of the history of Western philosophy and the resultant meaning of interpretation, or hermeneutics, as "retrieve." It will be helpful here to review this aspect of Heidegger's thought.

Recall that the historicality of man means that Being will disclose itself to him in different ways in different times, and that that disclosure will be limited by the time, and the language, within which Being discloses itself. Recall further that at the heart of Being is also negativity, at the heart of truth is also hiddenness, and that therefore every disclosure, or self-opening, of Being is also a withdrawal, or self-concealing, of Being at the same time. Recall finally that man is limited in his (linguistic) response to Being by the stage at which language has arrived at that time, so that language functions as fate for man's response to Being, i.e., it limits the response, and dictates the terms in which it can be made.

Now all of that means that there will be more to the disclosure of Being than can be expressed by language-fate in any given time. But recall also that the language of the response is elicited by Being, and is man's *response*. It is thus possible that more will have been elicited in that linguistic response than even the respondent was aware. That means it is possible to find more of the disclosure of Being in the words of a respondent of Being (a poet or "foundational thinker") than even he was aware. Thus, to read the words of a foundational thinker, to think after him his language, is to open oneself to the openness of Being which is hidden, even unsaid, in the language Being elicited from the foundational thinker. To do this is to "repeat" the thought and to "retrieve" the disclosure of Being granted to the thinker.[2]

The fact that Being conceals as it reveals, combined with the possibility of man to respond inadequately in thought/language to Being, has resulted in an increasing forgetfulness of Being in the history of Western philosophy. That philosophy, given birth by the wonder at Being by the earliest Greek thinkers, progressively lost that original insight, and began increasingly to consider beings in their various types and kinds. Thus, metaphysics, i.e., reflections on kinds of beings, results in "forgetfulness of Being," and the very success of philosophy with such "metaphysics" leads it farther and farther away from its original insight, i.e., wonder at Being. The task of the thinker is therefore to take a "step behind" metaphysics (the *Schritt zurück*), and get back to, "retrieve," the pristine wonder at Being itself. The thinker must thus retrieve the disclosure of Being granted to foundational thinkers, thereby stepping behind metaphysics to the origin of what degenerated into metaphysics, i.e., wonder at Being. The thinker must reclaim that original insight which was lost in the preoccupation of beings at the expense of Being. Therefore, if the self-disclosure of Being is to be responded to now, the thinker must expose himself to the language/thought response elicited by the self-opening of Being in the past, thereby responding in (contemporary) language/thought to that disclosure, bringing to light what the author himself could not see of that disclosure in his own response.[3]

All of this, it appears, is closely reflected in the way Fuchs traces the development of Christian thought and language, and the ensuing task of interpretation. In a variety of ways, Fuchs sketches out how the original event of Jesus became distorted, even forgotten, with the passage of time. Thus, with the passage of time, the Jesus-traditions were reworked from the vantage point of the story of the passion, and in the light of the proof texts from the Old Testament which had been developed by and for the kerygma. The result was that a kind of "apocalyptic biography" (i.e., the Gospels) of Jesus was produced. It was just this kind of apocalyptic viewpoint, with its expectation of the immediate return of Jesus, which caused the abandonment of the affirmation of the relevance of faith for the *present*; the locus of significance was shifted to the future.[4]

This falling away from the primal event was not due simply to carelessness or misunderstanding on the part of those early witnesses, however. It was, in fact, inevitable, as soon as it became apparent (as it did in Paul) that the earliest formulations of

Christian language needed to be interpreted. But as soon as that became necessary, that original language lost something of its truth, since the apostolic proclamation was never its precise equivalent. Thus, the very *proclamation* of the time-revelation of God in Jesus (i.e., Jesus' revelation that *now* was the time for the Kingdom, for love) altered the truth of that revelation, since by that proclamation revelation became a historical event. An example of the way that happened can be seen, Fuchs argues, in I Cor. 15:5–8, with its attempt to locate the resurrection historically (i.e., within history), which is quite different from the assertion that Christ died "for our sins" (I Cor. 15:3), something incapable of being thus located (or validated) historically. The very need to proclaim God's (unhistorical, i.e., not historically verifiable) revelation in Christ, therefore, forced that proclamation to turn the revelation into historical event.

Furthermore, the very success of that proclamation in creating a community of faith meant that faith would become, through this community, a historical phenomenon. But when that proclamation of Christ as the end of history thus became a historical entity, an alteration of the *content* of the proclamation was necessary in order to take that historical reality (the church) into account. Thus, despite the original insight that faith means a denial of all security within history, faith itself began to become a form of security within history because of its increasing success in relating itself to family, society, and state. The development of the church is thus the process of a twofold accommodation. On the one hand, it is the process of accommodating that original insight to the developing confession of faith which was compelled to take into account the success of the church as a historical entity. On the other hand, it is the process of accommodating the confession of faith to the original insight that was itself being altered, however, by its own historical success and development. There is thus a mutual influencing between world, in which the church succeeds, and in that way becomes a historical phenomenon, and faith, which must increasingly account for such historical success in historical terms. In that way the church itself could, and did, become a historical "security" for faith, thus robbing faith of its announcement of the danger of all such security.[5] In this process, then, the original understanding of faith was decisively altered.

The original understanding was not lost completely, however. The accommodation could never be totally successful. Therefore, it is possible to recover the original insight into the nature of God's revelation in Jesus, and thus of faith. It is for that purpose that historical research is necessary. Such historical research (the "retrieve" of the original response to the event of faith in Jesus!) discloses that the self-understanding of faith in the theology of the New Testament is opposed to the course of historical development which took place in the church.[6] Through historical research, therefore, we may get back to the truth of the original insight into the nature of faith, so long forgotten under the layers of historical development and mutual accommodation between world and proclamation.

Hermeneutic, therefore, is the attempt to retrieve that original insight into faith which has been obscured in the course of the development of the church, and its task consists in seeing that the language of faith does not become estranged from the language of the cross.[7] Hermeneutic must lead theology into the "step behind" its world- and history-encrusted language to the original language of the abandonment of self-assertion, i.e., to the language of the cross. The new hermeneutic, therefore, can be understood, it would seem, in terms of the "retrieve" of an original insight that later development, and necessarily so, caused to become obscure. The similarity to the Heideggerian position is quite clear: Heidegger's task is to retrieve the original insight (the wonder at Being) which the course of development of Western philosophy (metaphysics) has obscured, and to return philosophy to the language of Being by taking the step behind metaphysics, back to the original wonder at Being. By using this kind of thinking, the new hermeneutic can explain how the original view of cross and resurrection (i.e., the one found by the new hermeneutic) came to be distorted in the New Testament into something rather different.

This discussion has also led us to the point of being able to define the way in which the interpreter is to deal with Scripture. The interpreter must not be misled by attempts, present in Scripture, to interpret the Christian faith as, for example, a way of fathoming the plan history has followed, and will follow in the future. The interpreter must also be on his guard against the temptation, again present in Scripture, to ground faith in anything that itself is not faith. That is, the interpreter must judge the validity of the insight into the nature of faith, as it appears in a given text in the New Testament, to see whether or not that insight is pure, or whether it has been distorted. The interpreter must purify Scripture of those errors in the understanding of faith which could lead contemporary man astray in his search for the meaning of faith. The criterion by which the Scriptural understandings of faith are to be judged is clear: faith is a way of understanding the self as being free to live in love, i.e., free from the necessity of self-assertion as the means of securing the self in the world. Those portions of Scripture in which that understanding of faith is reflected thereby demonstrate the reliability of their stance vis-à-vis the original insight into the nature of faith, as that was announced by Jesus of Nazareth.

It will be instructive to see how this process works itself out in relation to specific Scriptural texts, and what the consequences of such a procedure are for an understanding of the historicality of human existence that makes such a procedure necessary. Because of the centrality of the witness to the resurrection for the New Testament, let us again choose it for our discussion.

When we deal with the accounts of the cross and resurrection, so it is argued, we are dealing with accounts of two qualitatively different events, when they are viewed from the perspective of history. The cross speaks of a man's death, an ordinary enough event, and one that is, at least in principle, open to verification by normal methods of historical investigation. No recourse to any categories beyond those normally employed in historical investigation will be needed to account for it. The resurrection, on the other hand, speaks of life after death, something decidedly uncommon in normal human experience, and something that is not open to historical verification in any normal way. In fact, the accounts of the resurrection imply that the cause of this event is the direct act of God in raising Jesus from the dead, a category of cause and effect not available to the historian in any normal pursuit of his evidence.

That means that knowledge of the resurrection is open only to faith. It is not something outside of faith upon which faith could be based; it is something available only in and to faith. "That means for the resurrection," writes Fuchs, "that one can only risk belief in Jesus' resurrection if he will risk, as Jesus did, claiming that God's grace is God's true will, and hold fast to it even to death. The risk is and remains something *risked*. . . . The true help of faith lies in itself." As a result, one must say of the New Testament witness to the resurrection: "For that reason, the message of Jesus' resurrection remains basically a statement of faith, which is believed 'with the heart' or it is not believed."[8]

There is, of course, some rather specific evidence in the New Testament witness to the resurrection that points in exactly the opposite direction. There is, for example, much that places the cross and resurrection on the same level, so far as faith is concerned. That is, no distinction is made between the availability of knowledge of the cross by ordinary means, and of the resurrection only by faith. Both belong, on equal terms, in the confession of faith (cf. I Thess. 4:14), and both must be equally proclaimed, again in the same terms (cf. I Cor. 15:3–4, where death and resurrection are mentioned in parallel formulas, and are cited as the content of apostolic proclamation in v. 11b). Apparently, the relation of faith to Jesus' death and to his resurrection is the same. That is, the meaning of both is open to faith.

The point at issue is thus not the event-character of the one or the other, nor is the resurrection spoken of as the object of faith in a way the death is not (cf. Rom. 5:6, 8, 10; 6:10; 8:32; 14:9, 15; I Cor. 8:11; II Cor. 5:14–15; I Thess. 5:10). It is further clear that the resurrection of Jesus as such is not the object of faith, nor for that matter, does proclamation of the resurrection intend to lead to faith in itself, nor even in Jesus; it leads to faith in God. That is true for Paul (Rom. 4:24) as well as for other, later authors (Col. 2:12; I Peter 1:21). In this light, it is clear that even in Rom. 10:9, the emphasis lies on God who raised Jesus from the dead, not, as Fuchs seems to assume, on the fact of the resurrection as such.[9]

This view is then retained in the sermons in Acts, where proclamation of God's having raised Jesus from the dead (chs. 2:24; 3:15; 4:10; 5:30; 10:40; 13:30; 17:31), of which the apostles are witnesses (chs. 4:33; 5:32; 10:41; 13:31; cf. I Cor. 15:3 ff.), leads not to a call to believe that Jesus rose from the dead, but to a call to *act* appropriately in the light of the resurrection, i.e., to repent and be baptized. The decision does not consist, in these instances, in deciding to believe *in* the resurrection; rather, it consists in deciding to act appropriately *because* of it. The resurrection is here not the *object* of faith, it is the *basis* of faith as a way of meeting life! Finally, in the account of the confrontation between Jesus and Thomas in John 20:26 ff., the content of Thomas' confession is not that Jesus has risen from the dead, but rather that the now-risen Jesus is his "Lord and God" (v. 28). *That* is the confession which those who have not seen will make, and be blessed for it, *not* that Jesus rose from the dead. Thomas has just *seen* (indeed, verified!) that; it is the *basis* for his paradigmatic confession of faith.

This is also the case with Paul when he writes to the Christians at Corinth. What could he mean but that the resurrection is the basis of faith when he writes, "If Christ is not risen, your faith is foolishness" (I Cor. 15:17), a point he had made shortly before not only about faith but also about preaching (v. 14). That repetition seems to indicate he meant to say just that. And the point Paul makes, clearly, is that the resurrection is not an object of faith, it is the basis of faith; it is, in fact, the kind of event about which knowledge can be gained from eyewitnesses.

That, rather obviously, is directly counter to the view of faith held by the new hermeneutic. How is such a conflict to be resolved? Easily enough; it is Paul who has erred here. He has been led into the kind of statement about faith that he cannot responsibly make. As to why Paul made such a statement, there are several answers. For one, it can be argued that Paul was led into a polemical misstatement of his own position, that he realized it, and then "corrected" it in I Cor. 15:20–28 by putting the resurrection again within the context of faith.[10] For another, it can be argued that those statements resulted from Paul's having misunderstood the position of his Corinthian opponents. They, as Gnostics, Fuchs suggests, may well have argued, not that the resurrection would not occur, but that their resurrection had occurred already.[11] Just why a misunderstanding of an opponent's position should invalidate a statement Paul makes about the relationship between faith and resurrection is not clear. Did Paul change his mind about the nature of faith, as the position of his opposition changed? Or would he have changed his mind about faith, had he realized the true nature of the opposition? Or, had he realized his opponents' position, would he not have said it quite *that way*? One gets the impression that the new hermeneutic would have much preferred that the latter in fact have been the case![12]

A further indication of the extent to which Fuchs finds I Cor. 15:14, 17, difficult for his position is indicated, I think, by the fact that in his essay on I Cor., ch. 15, he nowhere mentions, even by number, either of these two verses. They appear buried, as it were, in vs. 12–19, which are mentioned, but only in passing, as something that could be understood "without any faith at all."[13] That, obviously, is the whole difficulty with these verses, as far as Fuchs is concerned.

Paul, in short, has, according to the view of the new hermeneutic, included, however provoked, an element of "unfaith" in his discussion, seeking to ground the faith in some guarantee that was valid apart from faith. Paul's "true" position, so it is argued, is seen in I Cor. 15:11, where Paul shows he really thought faith preceded any "seeing" because he mentions proclamation before he mentions faith. Or it can be seen that Paul must have thought knowledge of the resurrection depended on faith because before he "saw" Jesus risen, Fuchs urges, he had already "stood under the influence of the proclamation of the Christians he persecuted."[14] Whether that is more convincing evidence than the twofold basing of faith on resurrection found in I Cor. 15:14, 17, the reader will have to decide. It must also be noted that this way of understanding the relationship of "faith" and "seeing" denies the evidence that Paul was decidedly not "within" the faith when Jesus appeared to him (cf. I Cor. 15:8 f.; Gal. 1:13 ff., and esp. v. 12!), and seems to want to repristinate a view, now generally discarded, that Paul's conversion (the resurrection "appearance") was the result of, and prepared for by, pressures, psychological and otherwise, exerted on Paul as a young Jew by the Christians whom he persecuted.

In this way, in any case, the new hermeneutic attempts to defend a view of faith, based on some portions of the New Testament, from a view of faith based on other portions. It is further clear that the view of faith that is rejected is one that sees God at work in history in such a way that he is seen as the "cause" of certain historical "effects," e.g., the resurrection of Jesus from the dead. Such a view, it is argued, is no longer tenable because to understand God's way of working in such terms is to think mythologically, and such thinking is no longer possible for man in the twentieth century. However valid it may have been for first-century man—and even for him its appropriateness is disputed—to regard it as valid now is to overlook the historically conditioned nature of human thought. It is to deny the historicality of man's response to his world in terms of the language and world view available to him in any given period. Unless, therefore, one gives up the idea of God working within history, he will be accused of having attempted the importation of ancient thought-categories into modern times, thus denying the historicality of human existence.

It is also clear, however, that the view of faith defended by the new hermeneutic is regarded as being the "true" or "valid" view of faith *in the New Testament* as well. In their best moments, this is the view of faith recognized as valid by Paul and John, especially, but also by some other New Testament authors.

This was Bultmann's argument in his essay on demythologizing; he was simply carrying to its conclusion the reinterpretation of myth begun already by John and Paul. This is also the position of Fuchs, who can assert that from the beginning, myth was an enemy of the gospel, and was never appropriate as a means of expressing the truth of faith. That is to say, the view of faith that is acceptable to modern man, i.e., demythologized, is also the view of faith that the New Testament authors, in their best moments, also held. Fuchs is quite explicit on that point. The same decision is required of us now as was required of the followers of Jesus of Nazareth. There is no difference, "faith is always the same."[15] That New Testament faith, furthermore, was intended to answer the question about the self, precisely the question that is still basic for man in the twentieth century. Thus faith, always the same, answers the question that has always been man's primary concern, namely, the question of the self. For that reason, the question of the self is the only question that can serve as the hermeneutical principle, by means of which the intention of the text can be laid bare.

But what now with the historicality of human existence? If this is the view of faith operative in the first century, is not the historicality of man and his historically conditioned way of thinking denied if it is also accepted as the view of faith that can operate now? Is not the assertion that the central problem of modern, Western, technological man was also the central problem of primitive, Eastern, agricultural, pre-scientific man, in itself a denial of that historicality, that time-conditionedness of human life and thought? Or does man remain thus unchanged and unchanging? If he does, how can we really speak of the "historicality of existence" in any serious way? If he does remain so much the same, can we really affirm that language, which changes and grows, really plays any significant part in shaping man? But if man does change, then how can an analysis of the way human existence is understood *now* (e.g., Heidegger) provide us with the tools of interpreting the way human existence was understood *then*? How can such an analysis provide us with the key able to unlock the true concern, and understanding of existence, which informed the myths of the first-century Hellenistic world? If, on the other hand, it is possible that a view of faith valid in the first century can still be valid now, then why is it not possible that the view of faith which sees God at work in history could also provide a possible alternative? Is the real reason for preferring the former over the latter to be found in the fact that the former view, i.e., faith concerned with the question of the self, is in fact read back into the text? But is it then "interpretation" in any acceptable form of the word, to "find" that view as one among others in the New Testament?

We face, in short, something of a dilemma in the new hermeneutic. If the modern view of faith is identical with the view, the "true" view, of faith in the New Testament, then has not the historicality of human existence really been ignored? If, on the other hand, that historicality is preserved, and the modern view of faith is not identical to that of the New Testament, but is based on the modern problem of the identity crisis of the individual in modern technological society, then is not the attempt to import it into, and then find it in, the New Testament, really to give up any serious attempt at interpretation? It would appear that it is difficult to affirm in any serious way the historicality of human existence, linked to and affected by the growth and change of language and of history, *and* at the same time to affirm that the understanding of faith in terms of the question of the self remains unchanged regardless of historical period or stage of linguistic heritage.

However that problem may be resolved, certain points with which the new hermeneutic concerns itself are of central importance for any serious consideration of the Christian faith. Surely the assertion that faith is a way of meeting life, rather than the provision of esoteric knowledge, *must* be taken seriously. Surely the question of finding the correct hermeneutical principle *must* be solved. Surely the problem of the self *must* be a concern for any modern attempt to speak relevantly of the meaning of faith.

Yet any attempt to speak of New Testament faith will surely have to come to terms with the New Testament witness to Christ risen from the dead more effectively than has the new hermeneutic. Any attempt to understand the Christian faith as a way of reacting to life will surely have to take seriously the challenge of finding in the Biblical style of life, resources for meeting the problems of life in the twentieth century, problems that are not dealt with by the first-century authors of the New Testament. Any concern for a modern understanding of faith must surely take seriously the continuity of the community of faith within which man may come to understand, and solve, the problem of the self.

We end our reflections, then, not with an answer, but with questions; not with a solution, but with problems. For the present, however, that may have to be the more appropriate stance for those who are committed to, and who would take seriously the meaning of, the Christian faith in the twentieth century.

Notes

CHAPTER 1. THE SHAPE OF THE PROBLEM

1. Cf. the *New Schaff-Herzog Encyclopedia of Religious Knowledge* (Funk & Wagnalls Company, 1910), Vol. 4, pp. 237 ff., where the article is entitled "Exegesis or Hermeneutics."

2. The renewed interest in hermeneutics as a theological problem is demonstrated by the fact that whereas in the first edition (1910) of *Die Religion in Geschichte und Gegenwart*, a basic theological reference work in German, the article entitled "Hermeneutik" consisted of three lines, in the third edition of that work (1959) it comprises some twenty columns.

3. The word "modern" is being used here in contrast to "ancient" and "medieval."

4. Cf. Ernst Fuchs, *Hermeneutik*, 3d ed. (hereafter cited as *Herm.*) (Bad Cannstatt: R. Müllerschön Verlag, 1963), p. 162.

5. Carl E. Braaten, *History and Hermeneutics* (New Directions in Theology Today, Vol. II) (The Westminster Press, 1966), p. 52.

6. In much of what follows, those who are familiar with Gerhard Ebeling's article "Hermeneutik," in *Die Religion in Geschichte und Gegenwart*, 3d ed. (Tübingen: J. C. B. Mohr, 1959), Vol. III, coll. 242–262, will recognize my debt to him.

7. Friedrich Schleiermacher, *Hermeneutik und Kritik mit besonderer Beziehung auf das Neue Testament*, ed. by Fr. Luecke (Berlin: G. Reimer, 1838). The book was not originally written as a book, but was assembled after Schleiermacher's death by the editor from written lecture notes left behind by Schleiermacher, and from notes recorded by students who heard that series of lectures on hermeneutics.

8. Karl Barth, *Epistle to the Romans*, tr. by E. C. Hoskyns (London: Oxford University Press, 1950), p. 8.

9. This is of course the point of "demythologizing." We shall have more to say about Bultmann in Chapter Four.

10. An example of this is the comment R. Grob makes in his treatment of the very difficult account of the healing of a deaf-mute by Jesus. His "interpretation" of Mark 7:33a ("And taking . . . [the deaf-mute] aside from the multitude privately") is: "When the Lord desires us to be the recipients of a miracle, he takes us away to a personal encounter with himself." If only interpretation could be done that easily! (*Einführung in das Markusevangelium*, p. 104; Stuttgart: Zwingli Verlag, 1965.)

11. René Marlé, S. J., *Introduction to Hermeneutics* (Herder & Herder, Inc., 1967), p. 113. The author devotes a chapter, "The Problem of Hermeneutics and Catholic Theology," to this discussion. Cf. also Gerhard Ebeling, "The Significance of the Critical Historical Method for Church and Theology in Protestantism," in *Word and Faith*, tr. by J. W. Leitch (London: SCM Press, Ltd., 1963), pp. 17 ff., for a discussion of the Roman Catholic solution from a Protestant viewpoint.

12. This is, of course, the position sketched out by Karl Barth in the Preface to the first edition of his commentary on Romans, written in 1918 (*The Epistle to the Romans*, tr. by E. C. Hoskyns, pp. 1 f.; London: Oxford University Press, 1950).

13. James Robinson, "Theology as Translation," in *Theology Today*, Vol. 20 (1963–1964), p. 522.

CHAPTER 2. MARTIN HEIDEGGER—I

1. Perhaps the most thorough treatment of Heidegger's thought in English is the massive book by Wm. J. Richardson, *Heidegger: Through Phenomenology to Thought* (The Hague: Martinus Nijhoff, 1963). A somewhat simpler treatment, depending more on Heidegger's earlier writings, especially his *Sein und Zeit* (*Being and Time*, see note 5), is the book by J. J. Kockelmanns, *Martin Heidegger: A First Introduction to His Philosophy*, tr. by A. S. and T. Schrynemakers and H. J. Koren (Duquesne University Press, 1965).

2. Martin Heidegger, *Sein und Zeit*, Vol. VIII of *Jahrbuch für Philosophie und phänomenologische Forschung*, ed. by E. Husserl (1927; currently published in Tübingen: Max Niemeyer Verlag, 1963), p. 35. *Being and Time*, tr. by J. Macquarrie and E. Robinson (London: SCM Press, Ltd., 1962), p. 60.

3. Martin Heidegger, *Unterwegs zur Sprache* (Pfullingen: Neske Verlag, 1960), pp. 241, 11, respectively.

4. There are other structural elements analyzed by Heidegger which we have not discussed, such as "being-in" and "being-with," but we have treated enough of them, I think, to give some indication of what Heidegger is up to. This discussion, like all that precedes

and follows in this chapter and the next, is rather drastically simpli-
fied—oversimplified, some will feel, I am sure—but our purpose is
to illustrate a type of thinking that is important for the new hermeneutic, not to give a thorough treatment of Heidegger's philosophy.

5. This, of course, explains the title of Heidegger's book *Being
and Time*. If man is the place where Being comes to light, and man
is basically temporal in structure, then the framework, the dimen-
sion, within which the question of Being arises is time. The second
volume of that work, to be entitled *Zeit und Sein* (Time and
Being), although projected, was never published.

Chapter 3. Martin Heidegger—II

1. Discussion of "truth" is not, of course, limited to the "later"
Heidegger; its main outlines were already present in the book *Being
and Time*. We have reserved it for treatment here because it seemed
an appropriate way to show how the concept of "Being" evolves in
the later thought of Heidegger, and also to show how the later
thought has its roots in the earlier discussions.

2. See §44 in *Being and Time*, for a basic discussion of "truth."

3. I owe this phrase, along with much else, to Wm. J. Richardson,
Heidegger: Through Phenomenology to Thought, p. 608.

4. For example, *Unterwegs zur Sprache*, p. 30.

5. *Ibid.*, p. 166.

6. It is for this reason that Heidegger feels free to carry on the
kind of etymology that he does. To be bound in etymology to the
historical meaning of roots is precisely to ignore the historical structure of Being. Unless an etymology is "forced" in this sense, it
reveals no new perspective, which the sheer historical development
of language as response to Being would demand. Thus, if "hermeneutics" is derived from the name of the Greek god of communication, Hermes, something which historically was (probably) not the
case, it can be legitimated by the necessity of retrieving for our time
the event of Being crystallized originally in the Greek word *hermēneuein*. The nature of thought, not historical philology, controls
such "etymologies."

7. For a discussion of the theological possibilities inherent in the
kind of thinking we have been describing in this chapter, cf. *The
Later Heidegger and Theology*, ed. by J. M. Robinson and J. B.
Cobb, Jr. (New Frontiers in Theology, Vol. I) (Harper & Row,
Publishers, Inc., 1963). For a negative evaluation, both of Heideg-
ger's philosophy and of its usefulness for theology, see Hans Jonas,
"Heidegger and Theology," in *Review of Metaphysics*, Vol. 18, No.

2 (December, 1964), pp. 207–233. Among other points, Jonas notes that there is no criterion in Heidegger's philosophy that allows one to determine which historic events are disclosures of Being, and which are not. Nor is there any way, in Heidegger's thought, to decide whether a positive or negative reaction to a given historic event is most appropriate. Jonas cites Heidegger's own response to National Socialism as an example.

CHAPTER 4. RUDOLF BULTMANN

1. Let mention of just two suffice, one by Giovanne Miegge, *Gospel and Myth in the Thought of Rudolf Bultmann,* tr. by S. Neill (John Knox Press, 1960); the other by B. H. Throckmorton, Jr., *The New Testament and Mythology* (The Westminster Press, 1959). The interested reader ought not be satisfied with secondary sources, however. Bultmann writes clearly enough so as to be readily understandable, even in translation.

2. Cf. Rudolf Bultmann, "Is Exegesis Without Presuppositions Possible?" in *Existence and Faith, Shorter Writings of Rudolf Bultmann* (hereafter cited as *E&F*), ed. and tr. by S. Ogden (The World Publishing Company, 1960), pp. 291 ff., and Rudolf Bultmann, *Jesus Christ and Mythology* (Charles Scribner's Sons, 1958), pp. 15 f., to give but two examples.

3. The first definition is found in Rudolf Bultmann, "The New Testament and Mythology," in *Kerygma and Myth* (hereafter cited as *K&M*), Vol. 1, tr. and ed. by R. Fuller (Harper & Row, Publishers, Inc., 1961), p. 10. For examples of the second definition, cf. "Bultmann Replies to His Critics" in *K&M*, p. 197; *Jesus Christ and Mythology*, p. 61.

4. *Jesus Christ and Mythology*, p. 84; cf. also "Bultmann Replies to His Critics" in *K&M*, pp. 210 f.

5. Virtually all the key points of the Heideggerian analysis of the structure of human existence turn up in Bultmann's writings. It belongs to man's nature to be related to himself (Rudolf Bultmann, *Theology of the New Testament,* Vol. I, tr. by K. Grobel, p. 196; Charles Scribner's Sons, 1951); man transcends himself by having his being in the future (*ibid.,* Vol. 1, p. 210); man is thrown into existence, i.e., receives his life from outside himself (*ibid.,* p. 218); man's selfhood is constituted by his decisions, whereby he gains or loses his selfhood (Rudolf Bultmann, *Jesus and the Word,* tr. by L. P. Smith and E. H. Lantero, pp. 52, 198, Charles Scribner's Sons, 1958; *History and Eschatology,* p. 44, Harper & Row, Publishers, Inc., 1957); death forces a man to come to grips with his

own selfhood (*Jesus Christ and Mythology*, p. 56), to cite but a few.

6. "Jesus and Paul" in *E&F*, p. 197.

7. "Bultmann Replies to his Critics" in *K&M*, p. 192; cf. also *Jesus Christ and Mythology*, pp. 44, 52 f.

8. On the whole question of approach to a text, see "Is Exegesis Without Presuppositions Possible?" in *E&F*, pp. 289 ff., and Rudolf Bultmann, "The Problem of Hermeneutics," in *Essays: Philosophical and Theological*, tr. by J. C. G. Greig (London: SCM Press, Ltd., 1955), pp. 234 ff. That this whole discussion of interpretation stands in closest relationship to Heidegger's thought ought to be so obvious as to make any need of demonstration superfluous.

9. It is apparent that Heidegger's thought about the "they" who take over the self is informing Bultmann's thought at this point.

10. Cf. *Jesus and the Word*, pp. 211 ff.; *Theology of the New Testament*. Vol. 1, § 33, pp. 292 ff.

11. See *Jesus Christ and Mythology*, pp. 69 ff., as an example of this position.

12. "Jesus and Paul" in *E&F*, p. 197.

13. *Jesus and the Word*, p. 54.

14. Although we have not attempted to indicate that fact, much of Bultmann's work has been of an exegetical nature, and he normally gives the New Testament passages which he believes not only legitimate, but even demand, the kind of interpretation he gives to them. His favorite authors are Paul and John, who he feels took the step in the direction which made demythologizing necessary.

15. On this last point, cf. *Jesus Christ and Mythology*, p. 77; "The Historicity of Man and Faith" in *E&F*, pp. 107 ff.; *History and Eschatology*, p. 44. For a broader discussion of this whole problem, cf. "The New Testament and Mythology" in *K&M*, esp. the latter portion of that essay, and "The Historicity of Man and Faith" mentioned above, as well as "Bultmann Replies to His Critics," also in *K&M*.

16. Cf., for example, "The Concept of Revelation in the New Testament," in *E&F*, esp. p. 79.

17. That Bultmann has retained this position despite all criticism is apparent in "The Primitive Christian Kerygma and the Historical Jesus" (*The Historical Jesus and the Kerygmatic Christ*, ed. and tr. by C. E. Braaten and R. A. Harrisville, pp. 15-42; Abingdon Press, 1964).

18. These phrases appear in Bultmann's essay on demythologizing ("The New Testament and Mythology" in *K&M*) but can be duplicated in many of his writings.

19. As Bultmann does, for example, in *Jesus Christ and Mythology*, pp. 68 f.

CHAPTER 5. LANGUAGE, PERCEPTION, AND REALITY

1. I have drawn this example, as well as many others, from *Psychology of Perception*, by William Dember (Holt, Rinehart and Winston, Inc., 1966), pp. 278 ff. When the inferences drawn from such experiments differ from those presented by Dember, it will be clearly indicated. It would be unfair to him to make him bear responsibility for a layman's conclusions.

2. Dember, *op. cit.*, pp. 312 f.

3. *Ibid.*, p. 210.

4. Reported in R. Kwant, *The Phenomenological Philosophy of Merleau-Ponty*, tr. by H. J. Koren and J. R. Kanda (Duquesne University Press, 1963), p. 41.

5. Cf. Dember, *op. cit.*, p. 193.

6. Cf. *ibid.*, pp. 190-192.

7. Reported in *ibid.*, pp. 238 ff.

8. Discussed in *ibid.*, pp. 262 ff.

9. W. H. Ittelson and F. P. Kilpatrick, "Experiments in Perception," in *Scientific American*, Vol. 185, No. 2, pp. 50-55; cited in Dember, *op. cit.*, pp. 263 f. The quotation is taken from p. 55 of the article, cited on p. 267 in Dember, *op. cit.* The French philosopher Merleau-Ponty came to the same conclusion; his views are summarized in Kwant, *op. cit.*, p. 164.

10. For a discussion of a person injured in wartime, who lacked the ability to arrange his total perceptual field into a unity, see the discussion of the "Schneider case" in Kwant, *op. cit.*, pp. 39 ff.

11. The subject is seated in a darkened room, in which an illumined rod and square are visible, the rod inside the square. The subject is told to place the rod in a verticle position. Some rely on the square, which has been tilted to one side, whereas others ignore the erroneous visible reference (the square), and, of course, come closer to verticle than the first group. Reported in Dember, *op. cit.*, p. 229.

12. For a highly readable and provocative discussion of this whole problem, see Owen Barfield, *Saving the Appearances* (Harcourt, Brace and World, Inc., n. d.).

13. Reported in Dember, *op. cit.*, p. 302.

14. Dember, *op. cit.*, p. 299.

15. *Ibid.*, pp. 320 f.

16. Reported in *ibid.*, pp. 290 ff.

17. With this distinction between "reality" and "real," I am pointing to the difference between what is "out there" apart from perception (the "real") and the way we perceive it, with all the limiting and organizing aspects imposed on it by our sensory organs and the various contexts within which perception takes place ("reality").

18. On this point, cf. Barfield, *op. cit.*, pp. 28 ff.

19. For an excellent discussion of the place and importance of language for man and his world, see Georges Gusdorf, *Speaking (La Parole)*, tr. by P. Brockelman (Northwestern University Press, 1965).

CHAPTER 6. MAN AND LANGUAGE

1. Cf. Fuchs, *Herm.*, pp. 99 ff.

2. In the light of that influence, it should not be surprising to learn that the method to be followed is that of phenomenology; cf. Ernst Fuch, *Marburger Hermeneutik* (hereafter cited as *MH*) (Tübingen: J. C. B. Mohr, 1968), p. 7.

3. Cf. Ernst Fuchs, "The New Testament and the Hermeneutical Problem" in *The New Hermeneutic*, ed by J. M. Robinson and J. B. Cobb, Jr. (Harper & Row, Publishers, Inc., 1964), Vol. II in the series New Frontiers in Theology, p. 117. The whole adaptation of Heidegger's concepts for theological reflection which was carried out by Bultmann is here presumed.

4. Cf. Fuchs, *MH*, p. 15.

5. Cf. Gerhard Ebeling, *The Nature of Faith*, tr. by R. G. Smith (Muhlenberg Press, 1961), p. 124; Fuchs, *Herm.*, pp. 194 f.

6. This is a favorite phrase of Fuchs's; cf. for example, *Herm.*, pp. 156 ff.

7. Ebeling, *Nature of Faith*, p. 180.

8. *Ibid.*, p. 115; cf. also Fuchs, *Herm.*, p. 133.

9. Cf. Fuchs, *Herm.*, p. 66. Fuchs feels he has here gone beyond Bultmann, who, says Fuchs, was not always clear on what the structural implications of "decision" are, i. e., what all is decided in that one decision.

10. Cf. Fuchs, *MH*, p. 241.

11. Fuchs, *MH*, pp. 34 f.

12. Fuchs himself draws this inference (*Herm.*, p. 139).

13. Cf. Ebeling, *Nature of Faith*, pp. 188 f.; also his article "Word of God and Hermeneutic" in *The New Hermeneutic*, ed. by Robinson and Cobb, pp. 93 f. It may also be noted that while "word-event" and "language-event" mean virtually the same, Ebe-

ling uses the former (*Wortgeschehen*) and Fuchs the latter (*Sprachereignis*).

14. Cf. Fuchs, *Herm.*, pp. 68 f.

15. Cf. also *ibid.*, p. 63; Ebeling, *Nature of Faith*, p. 188.

16. Cf. Fuchs, *Herm.*, p. 136.

17. Cf. *ibid.*, pp. 126 ff. I have attempted to rephrase the basic lines of argumentation as he presents them there. In the absence of any differentiation between "reality" (as the organized totality within which man exists) and the "real" (as what is "out there," whether it is incorporated into that totality or not), I have interpreted "reality" here in terms of the Heideggerian use of the word "world." Further, Fuchs uses the word "reality" in ways similar to the way Heidegger speaks of "Being"; e. g., reality depends on language; the "truth" of reality is possible only through language (p. 134); language "frees" reality (p. 130); etc. For a somewhat different approach to the problem, see Fuchs's discussion of the dependence of reality on time, and man's ability, given through language which is predicated on time (e.g., the tenses), to place reality at his own disposal (e. g., "Alte und neue Hermeneutik" in *Glaube und Erfahrung* (hereafter cited as *GuE*) (Tübingen: J. C. B. Mohr, 1965), pp. 227 ff. This is the third volume of his collected essays.

18. Fuchs, "The New Testament and the Hermeneutical Problem," in *The New Hermeneutic*, ed. by Robinson and Cobb, pp. 125 f.

19. Cf. on this usage Fuchs, *MH*, esp. pp. 175 f., 241 ff.

20. This is a theme upon which Fuchs plays almost endless variations. Since it occurs throughout his writings, we will limit ourselves to citing certain passages by way of example: the idea that in language, the self grants room for others (*MH*, p. 178); that language creates community (*Herm.*, p. 137 *et passim*); that language is the way the self grants itself to another ("Alte und neue Hermeneutik," in *GuE*, p. 212); that language "imparts" ("What Is a Language Event?" in *Studies of the Historical Jesus*, tr. by A. Scobie, p. 210; London: SCM Press, Ltd., 1964); that language is the arena of love, peace, and joy ("Alte und neue Hermeneutik," in *GuE*, p. 214).

21. On this whole discussion of word as event, cf. Ebeling, *Nature of Faith*, pp. 87, 185 ff., and "The Word of God and Hermeneutic," in *The New Hermeneutic*, ed. by Robinson and Cobb, p. 103. The quotation in this paragraph is from *Nature of Faith*, p. 186.

22. Ebeling, *Nature of Faith*, p. 90.

23. Ebeling, "Word of God and Hermeneutic," in *The New*

Hermeneutic, ed. by Robinson and Cobb, p. 100; cf. also pp. 101 ff. See also Fuchs, *Herm.,* p. 71, where the "inner impulse of language" is "the impulse of the word of God."

24. Fuchs, "Alte und neue Hermeneutik," in *GuE,* p. 226.

25. Fuchs, "Hermeneutik?" in *GuE,* p. 131.

26. Fuchs, *MH,* p. 203.

27. We use "presence" here to translate the German word *Gegenwart,* which can mean "present" in the temporal as well as spatial sense. This dual meaning is implied when we speak of language conferring "presence."

28. Fuchs, *Herm.,* p. 175.

29. *Ibid.,* p. 169.

30. *Ibid.,* p. 176.

31. Cf. Ebeling, "The Word of God and Hermeneutic," in *The New Hermeneutic,* ed. by Robinson and Cobb, p. 109; Fuchs, "The New Testament and the Hermeneutical Problem" in *ibid.,* p. 141.

32. Fuchs, "Das Wesen des Sprachgeschehens und die Christologie," in *GuE,* p. 232.

CHAPTER 7. FAITH

1. So Fuchs, *Herm.,* pp. 124, 189. This latter assertion Fuchs claims to be the position of Paul as reflected, for example, in I Cor. 11:31 ff.

2. Ebeling, *Nature of Faith,* pp. 56, 114. Ebeling finds this faith concretely expressed in Jesus' saying about not being anxious (Matt. 6:25 ff.).

3. Ebeling, *Nature of Faith,* p. 168.

4. *Ibid.,* pp. 164 f.

5. Fuchs, *Herm.,* pp. 187 ff. This, argues Fuchs, is the purpose of the Pauline letters; they are "illumination of existence" in the light of the "truth of faith."

6. Ebeling, *Nature of Faith,* p. 25. He cites Abraham as an example of this on p. 27.

7. *Ibid.,* p. 169.

8. Fuchs, *Herm.,* p. 265.

9. Fuchs, *MH,* p. 123; cf. also Ebeling, *Nature of Faith,* p. 159.

10. Ebeling, *Nature of Faith.,* pp. 170 ff.

11. This is a recurring theme in the writings of Fuchs. Cf. "Das Wesen des Sprachgeschehens in der Christologie," in *GuE,* esp. pp. 247 ff.; "Hermeneutik?" in *ibid.,* pp. 125 ff.; *Herm.,* pp. 269 f.

12. Fuchs cites the prodigal son as one who sought to put time at his own disposal (*Herm.,* pp. 269 f.).

13. Ebeling, *Nature of Faith,* p. 175.

14. The phrase is from *ibid.*, p. 181.

15. Cf. Fuchs, *Herm.*, p. 251. He cites II Cor. 5:17 as a basis for this remark.

16. Fuchs, *MH*, p. 197.

17. Cf. *ibid.*, p. 157, for this line of reasoning, which Fuchs holds to be a representation of the intention of the Gospel of John.

18. Fuchs, *MH*, p. 169.

19. This sentence is a close paraphrase of a sentence in Ebeling, *Nature of Faith*, p. 46; cf. also pp. 44 f., 166.

20. Fuchs, *Herm.*, p. 229. Fuchs uses the word *Einverständnis*, which we discussed in the previous chapter.

21. Fuchs, *Herm.*, pp. 112 ff., esp. p. 114.

22. The reader would not be far off the mark if he understood this analysis in terms of Heidegger's development of *das Man* ("they") and inauthentic existence, a fact that also accounts for its familiarity to those who are aquainted with Bultmann's analysis of man.

23. Fuchs, *Herm.*, p. 164.

24. *Ibid.*, p. 207. Fuchs argues that this tendency can be seen at work in such places as Matt. 24:37 to 25:46 and Luke 21:34-36. It also explains why apocalyptic and mythical imagery came to play as important a role in the writings of the New Testament as they did.

25. Fuchs, *Herm.*, pp. 147, 154.

26. Cf. *ibid.*, pp. 153, 265 ff.

27. Fuchs, *MH*, p. 181.

28. Cf. Fuchs, "Die Logik des Paulinischen Glaubens," in *Geist und Geschichte der Reformation–Festschrift Hans Rückert*, ed. by H. Liebing and K. Scholder (Berlin: Walter de Gruyter and Co., 1966), p. 7; *Herm.*, pp. 156 f. *et passim.* In this article, Fuchs seeks to show that his position vis-à-vis *Heilsgeschichte* can be supported by the theology of Paul; hence the title, "The Logic of Pauline Faith."

29. Fuchs, *Herm.*, pp. 254 ff.

30. *Ibid.*, p. 241. Fuchs cites the theology of Oscar Cullmann as an example.

31. Fuchs, *Herm.*, p. 202.

32. Fuchs, *MH*, p. 19. This statement is made in direct contrast to the position of Wolfhart Pannenberg, whose position in this matter is, for Fuchs, clearly *anathema*; cf. also Fuchs, "Die Logik des Paulinischen Glaubens," in the Rückert *Festschrift*, p. 11, and his dispute with Prof. Walther Künneth in "Die Wirklichkeit Jesu Christi," in *GuE*, pp. 452-470.

33. E. g., Fuchs, *MH*, p. 151.

34. For the argument that prior to seeing the risen Christ, his power was opened to Paul by the presence of the believing community, cf. Fuchs, "Alte und neue Hermeneutik," in *GuE*, p. 215; that I Cor. 15:12-19 represents an element of unfaith, cf. *MH*, p. 129; that the resurrection appearances can be a problem for faith, cf. "Die Logik. . ." in the Rückert *Festschrift*, p. 9.

35. Cf. Ebeling, *Nature of Faith*, pp. 16, 178 ff.; Fuchs, "Das Wesen des Sprachgeschehens. . ." in *GuE*, p. 233.

36. Fuchs, "Kanon und Kerygma," in *Zeitschrift für Theologie und Kirche*, Vol. 63 (1966), pp. 422 f.; this last statement is based on Rom. 14:7-9 and 15:9-17; cf. also Ebeling, *Nature of Faith*, p. 169.

37. This is a close paraphrase of a sentence found in Fuchs, *Herm.*, p. 153.

38. Fuchs, *Herm.*, pp. 153 f., 271.

39. This relationship between the purpose of faith, and the inherent purpose of language itself, is so intimate that Fuchs can argue that faith simply follows the inner tendency of language itself. That tendency resides in the fact that language, containing as it does the possibility for the self to understand itself as something that is not to understand itself purely in terms of the world and its reality, challenges the man who is thus fallen, to become a self. That challenge, says Fuchs, is what grace is (cf. *Herm.*, p. 265). That is, language retains in itself the language-gain of those who have become selves, thus presenting man the possibility of himself becoming a true self. That this skirts dangerously close to finding a validation for faith in something that itself is not faith is, I think, rather apparent. It is a question whether or not the whole movement of the new hermeneutic may not be in danger, if not of validating faith itself, at least of validating its own approach to, and understanding of, faith, in this way. Whether or not that means they have succumbed to the temptation of validating faith by something outside of faith itself they will have to judge.

CHAPTER 8. THE APPROACH TO THE TEXT

1. These sentences are a rough paraphrase of the way Fuchs, in his first book on hermeneutic, begins his discussion in the section entitled "General Hermeneutic," and they seem as appropriate a way as any to get at the problem (*Herm.*, p. 103).

2. This is a close paraphrase of Fuchs's discussion in "Das Wesen des Sprachgeschehens und die Christologie," *GuE*, p. 241.

3. Cf. Fuchs, *MH*, pp. 244 f.

4. Fuchs, "Das Wesen des Sprachgeschehens. . . ," in *GuE*, p. 239.

5. Cf. Fuchs, *MH*, pp. 11, 37, 247.

6. Fuchs, "Das Wesen des Sprachgeschehens . . . ," in *GuE*, p. 246.

7. Fuchs, *MH*, p. 58. Fuchs cites II Cor. 6:3–10 as an example of such activity by Paul.

8. Cf. the famous dictum of Merleau-Ponty: "Something of the nature of the question passes into the answer" (*In Praise of Philosophy*, tr. by J. Wild and J. M. Edie, p. 14; Northwestern University Press, 1963).

9. Cf. H.-G. Gadamer, *Wahrheit und Methode*, 2d ed. (Tübingen: J. C. B. Mohr, 1965, pp. 277 f. For more on the hermeneutical circle as it applies to the new hermeneutic, cf. Fuchs, *Herm.*, pp. 120 ff.; *MH*, pp. 83 ff.; Gerhard Ebeling, "The Significance of the Critical Historical Method for Church and Theology in Protestantism," in *Word and Faith*, tr. by J. W. Leitch (London: SCM Press, Ltd., 1963), pp. 49 f., to mention but a few places.

10. Fuchs, *Herm.*, p. 122. Fuchs admits that not all NT texts lay such a necessity upon the interpreter, e.g., Acts or the Pastoral Epistles. It is true, however, he affirms, of Paul and the Gospel of John primarily, but also of the other Gospels as well. It is obvious that, for that reason, he regards these latter writings as more valuable, and as more closely related to what Jesus himself was about.

11. Fuchs, *Herm.*, pp. 155, 124 f.

12. Fuchs, *MH*, p. 211; *Herm.*, pp. 142 ff.

13. Fuchs, *MH*, pp. 39, 207; *Herm.*, p. 141.

14. Fuchs, *Herm.*, pp. 109 ff.

15. Fuchs, "Hermeneutik?" in *GuE*, p. 127.

16. Fuchs can refer to this as the "question about where" (*die "Wo-Frage"*); "Hermeneutik?" in *GuE*, p. 131. On pp. 127 ff. of the same article, he attempts to ground this by means of an exegesis of I Thess. 5:1–11. See also his *Herm.*, p. 111, and the discussion leading up to this conclusion.

17. Fuchs, "Die Logik des Paulinischen Glaubens," in the Rückert *Festschrift*, p. 5.

18. Fuchs, *Herm.*, p. 115.

19. *Ibid.*, pp. 116 f. The echoes of Heidegger are, I think, clear.

20. Fuchs, *Herm.*, p. 61.

21. Fuchs asks whether Rom. 7:24 could be the expression of such a hermeneutical principle, but then immediately points out that if such were the case, there would be no real problem with interpreting the New Testament. The existence of such problems of

interpretation indicates, Fuchs argues, that such a complaint, as is contained in Rom. 7:24, apparently *must* be misunderstood without further clarificatión, and therefore to claim it as the hermeneutical principle would be an act of self-deception (*Herm.*, pp. 111 f.).

22. See note 13 p. 124 for the distinction between "existenti*al*" and "existenti*ell.*"

23. Fuchs, *Herm.*, pp. 27 f.; cf. also pp. 147, 155. Those familiar with the theology of Wilhelm Herrmann will see here the affinities between his thought and that of Fuchs. Fuchs, of course, acknowledges that; cf. *Herm.*, pp. 36 f., 42 ff.; *MH*, pp. 95 ff., 102–112.

24. It is at this point, of course, that all theoretical discussions about language, translation, and interpretation become concrete, both for you, dear reader, and for me! How am I to be faithful to the free, poetic rendering which Fuchs gives these verses from Philippians? If I translate closely, the rhymes and rhythms are lost; if I preserve them, some accuracy is lost. So, I shall keep rhyme and rhythm, where possible those Fuchs uses; where not, I shall attempt to reproduce the "flavor" (hermeneutics, however theoretically and exactly begun, inevitably ends up using such inexact, analogous language!) of Fuchs's "song." The original appears as follows:

(6) Er war in Wahrheit ganz wie Gott
und wies als Raub von sich zurück,
Gott gleich zu sein.

(7) Allein,
um nichts davon an sich zu haben,
erwählt er sich des Sklaven Gaben
im Menschenschein.

(7b Als ihm dies Gleiches wie den Menschen bot,
8) gab er auch das noch hin,
gehorsam bis zum Tod,
zum Kreuzestod.

(9) Drum hob ihn auch Gott in die Höhe empor
und gab ihm den Namen im höchsten Chor:

(10) Im Jesuswort beuge sich jedes Knie
über Sternen, auf Erden, im Meer!

(11) Und keine Zunge, die da nicht schrie:
Jesus Christus ist *Herr!*
zu Gottes des Vaters vollkommener Ehr.

Herm., p. 104.

25. With this sentence we begin a translation of Fuchs, *Herm.*, pp. 105–107. Where it seemed advisable, I have explained or trans-

lated the Latin and Greek words Fuchs employs; in every instance, the Greek has been transliterated.

26. This is the end of the translation.

27. Fuchs, *Herm.*, p. 108.

28. That such an approach represents the application of Heideggerian thinking to the problem of interpreting the New Testament is, I think, clear.

CHAPTER 9. THE FIGURE OF JESUS

1. Fuchs, "Alte und neue Hermeneutik," in *GuE*, pp. 219 f.; "The New Testament and the Problem" in *The New Hermeneutic*, ed. by Robinson and Cobb, pp. 128 ff. In the former article, Fuchs cites the parable of the laborers in the vineyard (Matt. 20:1 ff.) as well as that of the prodigal son (Luke 15:11 ff.) as instances where this theme of understanding is treated. If the laborers had understood the situation, they would have anticipated what the Lord of the vineyard would answer to their objections (Matt. 20:13–15), and they could then themselves have reasoned their way to the conclusion that that Lord was generous and good, knowledge which in turn would have led them to rejoice. Understanding the situation allows one to participate in it, and allows it to be real for that person. This announcement of the present as the time of the coming of God's word then becomes the fundamental theme of the whole New Testament (so Fuchs, *Herm.*, p. 155).

2. Fuchs, "The New Testament and the Problem," in *The New Hermeneutic*, ed. by Robinson and Cobb, p. 130; "Language in the New Testament," in *Studies of the Historical Jesus*, tr. by Andrew Scobie (London: SCM Press, Ltd., 1964), p. 74.

3. Fuchs, *Herm.*, p. 227; "Alte und neue Hermeneutik," in *GuE*, p. 222.

4. Fuchs, "The New Testament and the Problem," in *The New Hermeneutic*, ed. by Robinson and Cobb, p. 123.

5. Fuchs, *Herm.*, p. 226; Ebeling, *Nature of Faith*, p. 55.

6. Cf. Fuchs, "Language in the New Testament," in *Studies of the Historical Jesus*, p. 73; *Herm.*, p. 139; "The New Testament and the Problem," in *The New Hermeneutic*, ed. by Robinson and Cobb, p. 131.

7. Fuchs, *Herm.*, p. 139; "Das Wesen des Sprachgeschehens und die Christologie," in *GuE*, pp. 242 f. Fuchs cites the antitheses of Matt. 5:21 ff. as an example of Jesus' language functioning in this way.

8. Fuchs, *Herm.*, p. 224.

9. Robert W. Funk, *Language, Hermeneutic, and Word of God* (Harper & Row, Publishers, Inc., 1966) p. 158. Funk's treatment of the parables is very illuminating, and is itself worth obtaining the book in order to read. It is the second of three sections in the book.

10. Cf. Fuchs, *MH*, pp. 232 f. In his discussion, Fuchs evaluates poetry the way Heidegger does, and argues that the parable functions the same way, and is thus a form of poetry.

11. Funk, *op. cit.*, pp. 155, 161. On an earlier page, Funk had written: "The burden of my contention is that what one sees is determined to no small degree by how he looks" (p. 126). In more technical terms, one can say that set, or context, influences perception. It may now be clear, if it was not before, why we felt it important to include a chapter on the nature of perception (Chapter 5, "Language, Perception, and Reality," above).

12. Fuchs, *Herm.*, pp. 223, 217; Funk, *op. cit.*, p. 162.

13. Fuchs, *Herm.*, p. 217; Funk, *op. cit.*, p. 143.

14. Funk, *op. cit.*, pp. 158 f., 135 f.; Fuchs, *Herm.*, p. 222; "Das Wesen des Sprachgeschehens . . . ," in *GuE*, p. 245. For that reason, Funk raises the question, relative to the *interpretations* of the parables in the Gospels (e.g., Matt. 13:36 ff.) "whether the church was justified in canonizing particular applications along with the parable itself" (*op. cit.*, p. 135, n. 11).

15. Fuchs, *Herm.*, pp. 224 f. That this whole manner of approaching and analyzing parables is quite different from that of, say, Joachim Jeremias (*The Parables of Jesus*, tr. by S. H. Hooke, rev. ed.; London: SCM Press, Ltd., 1963) ought to be rather obvious. The conclusions about the nature and purpose of the parables also differ, for the most part.

16. Cf. Fuchs, *Herm.*, pp. 219, 224; "Das Wesen des Sprachgeschehens . . ." in *GuE*, pp. 239 f.; Ebeling, *Nature of Faith*, p. 54.

17. Fuchs, "Das Wesen des Sprachgeschehens . . . ," in *GuE*, pp. 239 f.

18. Fuchs, "The New Testament and the Problem," in *The New Hermeneutic*, ed. by Robinson and Cobb, p. 133.

19. Ebeling, *Nature of Faith*, p. 60.

20. Fuchs, *Herm.*, p. 190. For a capsule summary of the necessity for, and the carrying out of, demythologizing, cf. Fuchs, *MH*, pp. 162 ff. The example used there is original sin, since that is one that Hans Jonas dealt with, and Fuchs is quoting and discussing Jonas. But the implications of that discussion are clear: any element of the original experience of faith that can, by being hypostasized, be accorded "objective" validity, whether in a historical or ontological sense, has thereby lost its original meaning, and has been trans-

formed into its opposite, i.e., it contributes to "worldly security" and self-assertion, rather than denial of such security and self in reliance on faith in God.

21. Fuchs, "Die Wirklichkeit Jesu Christ," in *GuE*, p. 467. It is recorded in John 20:4.

22. Fuchs, "Alte und neue Hermeneutik," in *GuE*, p. 215. Of the last three sentences, the first and third are close paraphrases of sentences of Fuchs's found in "Die Logik des Paulinischen Glaubens," in the Rückert *Festschrift*, p. 9.

23. Fuchs, *Herm.*, p. 157.

24. Fuchs, "Das Wesen des Sprachgeschehens . . . ," in *GuE*, p. 233.

25. Cf. Fuchs, "Die Logik . . . ," in the Rückert *Festschrift*, pp. 12 f.; "The NT and the Problem," in *The New Hermeneutic*, ed. by Robinson and Cobb, p. 136; Ebeling, *Nature of Faith*, p. 74.

26. Fuchs, *Herm.*, p. 145.

27. These sentences are a close paraphrase of material contained in Fuchs, *Herm.*, p. 229. Fuchs cites Phil. 3:10 when he says the power of the resurrection consists in the fact that the cross is proclaimed as comfort.

28. Fuchs, "Das Sprachereignis in der Verkündigung Jesu, in der Theologie des Paulus, und im Ostergeschehen," in *Zum hermeneutischen Problem in der Theologie* (hereafter cited as *Zum herm. Prob.*), 2d ed. (Tübingen: J. C. B. Mohr, 1960), p. 303.

29. Fuchs, *ibid.; Herm.*, p. 235. Ebeling has stated, in a similar vein, that to say "God" means to contradict the contradiction of God, namely, sin and death. Though God and death belong closely together, therefore, Ebeling affirms that to meet death does not mean to meet God, since life is the area of encounter with Him (*Nature of Faith*, pp. 75, 85). Fuchs can also associate God and death by arguing, for example, that love is fulfilled only where God appears, either in the word of faith or in death, yet it is clear that God is not to be equated simply with death, since for Fuchs, Jesus' resurrection can be stated simply by saying "Love never fails," and by his repeated assertions that God is love (cf. *MH*, pp. 6 f., 200, 251).

30. Cf. Fuchs, "Das Sprachereignis . . . ," in *Zum herm. Prob.*, p. 296; *Herm.*, pp. 209 f.

31. Fuchs, *Herm.*, pp. 246 f. In some instances, I have virtually reproduced Fuchs's language in translation. Cf. also, "Das Wesen des Sprachgeschehens . . . ," in *GuE*, pp. 234 ff.

32. Fuchs, "Das Wesen des Sprachgeschehens . . . ," in *GuE*, p. 235.

33. Cf. Fuchs, *Herm.*, p. 237; "Language in the New Testament," in *Studies of the Historical Jesus*, p. 80; "The Quest of the Historical Jesus," in *ibid.*, p. 28. In this last-mentioned passage, Fuchs cites Mark 8:34–38 as evidence that faith cannot be separated from suffering, and he cites Phil. 2:5–11 in the first-mentioned passage when he discusses the possibility of such selfhood becoming event in Jesus.

34. Fuchs, *Herm.*, p. 196.

35. *Ibid.*, p. 228.

36. Cf. Ebeling, "The Question of the Historical Jesus and the Problem of Christology," in *Word and Faith*, p. 304; Fuchs, "Kanon und Kerygma," in *Zeitschrift für Theologie und Kirche*, Vol. 63 (1966), p. 427; "Alte und neue Hermeneutik," in *GuE*, p. 227.

37. Fuchs, "Das Wesen des Sprachgeschehens . . . ," in *GuE*, p. 246; *Herm.*, p. 262. This points again to the theological necessity of the "new quest" of the historical Jesus; cf. "The Quest of the Historical Jesus," in *Studies of the Historical Jesus*, pp. 11–31.

38. Fuchs, *Herm.*, pp. 189, 258. Fuchs cites I Cor. 11:31 ff. re self-judgment; Phil. 2:2, 6–8, 12–18, re the unifying power of the Son's sacrifice.

39. Fuchs, *Herm.*, p. 195. Fuchs bases this exposition on Rom. 5:18 f.; 15:7; Phil. 2:6–8; I Cor. 5:7; 6:19; 15:21 f.; II Cor. 8:9.

40. Fuchs, *Herm.*, pp. 246 f., 155; "Alte und neue Hermeneutik," in *GuE*, p. 221; "Das Wesen des Sprachgeschehens . . . ," in *GuE*, p. 243.

41. Cf. "The NT and the Problem," in *The New Hermeneutic*, ed. by Robinson and Cobb, p. 127; *Herm.*, p. 71; "Das Sprachereignis . . . ," in *Zum herm. Prob.*, p. 295.

42. Cf. Fuchs, *Herm.*, pp. 269 f.; *MH*, pp. 48, 157; "The NT and the Problem," in *The New Hermeneutic*, ed. by Robinson and Cobb, pp. 134 f.

43. Cf. Fuchs, *MH*, pp. 216, 151; *Herm.*, p. 248; "Alte und neue Hermeneutik," in *GuE*, p. 230.

44. Fuchs, *Herm.*, p. 131; "Das Sprachereignis . . . ," in *Zum herm. Prob.*, p. 283.

45. Fuchs, "Alte und neue Hermeneutik," in *GuE*, p. 230.

CHAPTER 10. REFLECTIONS ON THE NEW HERMENEUTIC

1. This will of necessity be a rather "compact" discussion, and I shall not attempt to document statements with the frequency found in preceding chapters. I think the evidence cited there will uphold the validity of the present summary of the position of the new hermeneutic.

2. Heidegger's word, *Wiederholung*, can mean both "repeat" and "recover" or "retrieve"; this latter word is the one chosen by Wm. Richardson as most appropriate, and I shall follow that usage here (*Heidegger: Through Phenomenology to Thought*, p. 89, n. 181).

3. This carries as an obvious corollary the fact that to speak of the "refutation" of a foundational thinker is absurd. One can only ask how his response to Being may be understood and interpreted for a new time. Thought that is response to Being cannot be "wrong"; it is simply controlled by a fate-language different from our own.

4. Fuchs, *Herm.*, pp. 191, 208.

5. *Ibid.*, pp. 184 f., 266 f.

6. *Ibid.*, p. 270. The beginning of this development is given the name "early Catholicism," and explains why that phrase is such a term of opprobrium for some German New Testament scholars.

7. Fuchs, *Herm.*, p. 264.

8. "Die Frage nach dem historischen Jesus," in *Zur Frage nach dem historischen Jesus*, pp. 165, 163, respectively. For a rather different way of viewing, and understanding, the resurrection, cf. Wolfhart Pannenberg, *Jesus—God and Man*, tr. by L. L. Wilkins and D. A. Priebe (The Westminster Press, 1968), esp. Ch. 3, "Jesus' Resurrection as the Ground of His Unity with God" pp. 53 ff.; and Ch. 6, III, "Universal Conditioned Elements in Jesus' Activity," pp. 235 ff.

9. See note 8, above.

10. Fuchs, "Alte und neue Hermeneutik," in *GuE*, p. 216. Fuchs argues that Paul's statements in I Cor. 2:2 and Gal. 3:1 show the distortion contained in I Cor. 15:12–19.

11. Fuchs, "Die Auferstehungsgeswissheit nach I Korinther 15," in *Zum herm. Prob.*, p. 201. James M. Robinson has argued that Paul did know this to be their position, and that therefore these verses must be interpreted as arguing, not for resurrection per se, but for the final resurrection as still to come ("Kerygma and History in the New Testament," in *The Bible in Modern Scholarship*, ed. by J. Ph. Hyatt, pp. 121 ff.; Abingdon Press, 1965).

12. Fuchs, *MH*, p. 129.

13. Fuchs, "Die Auferstehungsgewissheit . . . ," in *Zum herm. Prob.*, p. 203.

14. Fuchs, "Das Sprachereignis . . . ," in *Zum herm. Prob., p.* 301.

15. Fuchs, *Herm.*, p. 266.

Index

SUBJECTS